Let's Make Money, Honey

THE COUPLE'S GUIDE TO STARTING
A SERVICE BUSINESS

**Barry Silverstein
and Sharon Wood**

⤢ GUIDE
WORDS

Cover image: Feng Yu/Shutterstock.com Author photo: Meghan Rolfe

GuideWords Publishing
5 Blue Damsel Court
Candler, NC 28715 USA
www.guidewords.pub
guidewordspub@gmail.com

Book Layout ©2013 BookDesignTemplates.com

Let's Make Money, Honey by Barry Silverstein and Sharon Wood—1st ed.
Library of Congress Control Number 2015946471
ISBN 978-0-9965760-0-0

Printed in the United States of America.

Contents

About this Book

Our objective in writing *Let's Make Money, Honey* is to discuss the unique aspects of running a business as a couple, as well as the special nature of running a service business. The book should be of value to two kinds of readers:

1. **Couples who are evaluating whether or not they want to start a service business together.** This book should help you determine if you have the skills to start a business as well as the "business compatibility" needed to work together.

2. **Couples who have already decided to take the plunge and start a service business together.** This book will function as your blueprint and show you what you need to do, step by step in sequence, to start and run a service business together. It will help minimize the risk associated with starting a new business.

Let's Make Money, Honey is relevant for any couple thinking about starting a service business together, but it should be especially pertinent to mature couples who may be looking for the "what's next" in their work lives and see real potential in being partners in a pre-retirement business.

As baby boomers, we started a business together later in life, after we already had successful careers and raised children. Our goal was to build a small pre-retirement business together and run it for a fixed period of time.

Here we tell the story of how we started and ran our service business and eventually sold it. You'll notice that we get into a significant amount of detail about the nitty-gritty of running our particular business. As you read the book, you may wonder why we spent time on details that seem to apply only to our business. When you understand at the detail level what it took for us to run our business, you'll be able to apply these experiences to your own business. What we went through is sure to be similar to the challenges you will face, because service businesses have a lot in common, especially in the way they treat customers as clients. In a service business, it's all about building client relationships.

Each chapter logically follows the other, showing the progression of the business. Most readers will derive the most benefit from the book by reading the chapters in order, but if you are just interested in certain aspects of running a service business and would like to skip around, that's okay too.

Chapters have a brief introduction – just scan the bulleted copy at the start of the chapter to learn about its basic content. At the close of each chapter is a section called "Consider This..." This is our take on the lessons you can take away from each chapter. We've also included "Lessons Learned" at the end of the book. This closing chapter should make the story of our particular business broadly applicable to any service business.

One last note about our voice: For the most part, we wrote as the collective "we" because our business operated as a very close partnership (we're married to each other and owned a business together). Still, there were many times we had to describe each other's distinct roles, so we "stepped outside ourselves" and wrote about each other from a comfortable distance. We thought this was important, since defining each person's individual responsibilities is a big challenge for couples who run a business together. It allowed us to make unique observations about each other's roles and reactions.

We hope you enjoy reading about our journey.

Love and Money

You're a couple in a loving relationship. You care about and support each other in your life's endeavors. Maybe you've wondered if you can translate the power of that personal relationship into a business relationship. Maybe you've even talked about running a business together. Maybe you've said to each other, not so jokingly, "Let's make money, honey."

The idea of starting and running a business together isn't for everyone: It is a unique escalation of a personal relationship that brings with it new and different kinds of pressure. The simple fact is it takes a special ability to be both life and business partners. Some couples could never imagine working with each other, while others are excited by the idea. Owning a business together is a phenomenon that is becoming more common – and when it succeeds, couples that are also business partners gain a new sense of joint pride and satisfaction.

Couples can decide to go into business together at any age. Some couples may have the entrepreneurial urge toward the beginning or in the middle of their careers. Others, like us, may find that being in business together is a viable encore career. Mature couples that tire of being in the workforce or leave jobs involuntarily could view a collaborative business as a fresh new opportunity to do something different and meaningful. Starting a business together later in life is a challenge, but it can be renewing and invigorating.

We really never thought about starting a business together until we decided to relocate and change our lifestyle. We had met at a company and worked together there. Our working relationship evolved into friendship, marriage, and then working together again at a company started by one of us.

The idea for starting a business as partners arrived fairly late in our lives. As baby boomers in our fifties with a daughter who was about to go off to college, we both wanted to find a way to exit our busy, stress-filled professions. We made a major life decision, left our jobs, and moved from New England to North Carolina. With both careers up in the air and a desire to be in charge of our own destiny, going into business together seemed to be a natural next step for us.

Apparently, we weren't the only boomers with entrepreneurial dreams. In 2013, for example, "businesses started by those ages 55 to 64 accounted for nearly one-quarter of all new businesses started," reported Dane Stangler, Vice President, Research and Policy of the Ewing Marion Kauffman Foundation in February 2014. Stangler added, "What might be more startling to many observers is that Americans in the 55 – 64 age group start new businesses at a higher *rate* than those in their twenties and thirties. This has been true, by the way, in every single year from 1996 to 2013." [1] Add this to the fact that family businesses make up over 80 percent of all business enterprises in North America [2] and starting a business as a couple looks pretty promising.

We're hopeful that our story will inspire couples with a desire to work together, regardless of age, to take the plunge – but to do so with their eyes wide open. It can be very fulfilling to both live together and work together in the same business, but as you'll see, doing so is not without its many challenges. In this book, we've mapped out exactly how we started our business, the steps we took to get it off the ground, and all the things we did to make it successful. We'll also tell you about the most surprising thing of all – how we ended up selling our business to a completely unexpected buyer.

But before you learn about the service business we ran together, we thought it might be useful to share the story of how we got there in the first place.

A DIRECT MARKETING LOVE STORY

We both worked for a firm that specialized in fund raising, Epsilon Data Management (Epsilon for short), in a city near Boston, Massachusetts. Barry had started Epsilon's corporate communications department, but after several years of running it, decided to leave to try his hand at being a creative director at a small ad agency. Sharon, meanwhile, was executive assistant to an Epsilon co-founder/senior vice president of marketing.

The department Barry left behind, now called marketing communications, needed a strong, competent manager, which turned out to be Sharon – so she ended up running the department that Barry started. But Barry realized that the agency he joined wasn't a good fit. Before he left, he called Epsilon's president for a reference. Instead of giving Barry a reference, the president urged him to return to the firm to head Epsilon's newly formed creative services department, so Barry came back.

Now the wheel of fate that would bring Barry and Sharon together took an interesting turn. Sharon's department needed to get copy and art produced for Epsilon's marketing materials. Barry's department served Epsilon's clients, but also had to meet the company's own needs. Sharon became an "internal client" of Barry's department, and the two managers began to work together.

To be honest, it wasn't love at first sight. In fact, Sharon says she often got the feeling Barry would run the other way when he saw her coming. It wasn't that he didn't like her (their later relationship would prove otherwise), it was that her projects were "non-revenue" related. As any agency creative director worth his salt will tell you, internal work takes a back seat to work from clients who are paying the bills. Still, these strange bedfellows (so to speak) had to work together. Along the way, they became friends.

Then Barry, always the entrepreneur, got the bug to do something different again. Epsilon had been successful servicing certain niches, expanding from its nonprofit base into frequent traveler programs and financial services. An untapped sector was technology, an area that intrigued Barry. This was at a time when information technology was booming in Massachusetts. Barry's idea was for Epsilon to service the high tech niche. Epsilon's management wasn't interested, however, so Barry began to think about a way to pursue the idea.

He decided he would start his own direct marketing agency to specialize in high tech, calling it "Directech," a name that represented "direct marketing for technology companies." He resigned from Epsilon in 1983 and opened a small office in Waltham, Massachusetts.

Barry left Epsilon, but he didn't lose touch with his friend Sharon. In fact, Sharon took an interest in Barry's fledgling agency. She would sometimes refer a prospect that was inappropriate for Epsilon to Barry, and one of those prospects became a client. To thank Sharon, Barry invited her to dinner.

Both of us had been recently divorced, so dinner turned out to be a bit more than business. In fact, that dinner was the beginning of a lasting relationship, one that led to marriage. We had Epsilon to thank for bringing us together, and when people asked how we met, we would tell them about our "direct marketing love story."

Turns out we had a kind of love affair with direct marketing as well. While Barry was building Directech, Sharon decided to make a move herself. She left Epsilon to take a job with a hot new direct marketing software company. Both of us were entrenched in the direct marketing industry but in different areas.

When we decided we wanted to have a child together, Sharon re-evaluated her job. We knew that, once she had a baby, it would make more sense for her to return to work part-time, but that wasn't an option her employer was willing to consider.

JOINING FORCES

That's when the thought occurred to us that the best solution to the problem could be for Sharon to work at Directech on a part-time basis. The agency was growing and Barry was handling all new business prospecting and presentations himself. Sharon was a skilled marketing and sales professional who knew the direct marketing business well. If she could lead the prospect generation and qualification effort, it would be a huge help. So we thought, why not join forces and work together?

The idea sounded good. We were already confident we could collaborate successfully at Directech because we had worked together at Epsilon. Barry was a conceptual, big idea person with creative writing ability. Sharon was a pragmatic, detail-oriented person with sales ability. Both of us were somewhat obsessive about work quality and deadlines. We had unique but complementary skill sets.

We did feel uncomfortable about one thing, though: the "boss's wife syndrome." We really didn't want an employee to be in the precarious position of getting caught between the two of us. We also didn't want any employee to report to Sharon, because they may have resented her part-time status. As a result, we carefully structured Sharon's job so it would be purely a new business function with no responsibility for existing client work. To make sure we were being completely objective about Sharon's position, Directech's Chief Operating Officer, not Barry, created and managed her compensation plan.

There was another more subtle aspect to Sharon's joining Directech: She retained her professional name, Sharon Wood. This helped maintain a psychological separation between us within the agency and, more importantly, outside the company. Again, we didn't want prospective clients or clients, for that matter, to be distracted by the fact that we were married.

We guarded the "secret" well; in many cases, prospects and clients had no idea we were husband and wife. This led to a few amusing occurrences. One time, a prospect off-handedly mentioned to Sharon, "You and Barry must know each other pretty well – you seem to complete each other's sentences." Another time, when we decided to treat ourselves to an overnight at a Cambridge hotel, we went down to brunch the next morning only to find, to our horror, a prospect of the agency seated at a nearby table. We didn't want the person to wonder what Directech's president and sales director were doing having brunch together on a Sunday, so we went over to the table to say hello. Sharon smiled and said, "You may not have known this, but Barry and I are married." That diffused what could have otherwise been an embarrassing situation.

WORK AND FAMILY: A DELICATE BALANCE

For the most part, being a husband and wife team at Directech was no problem for us or our employees. We did a good job defining our roles and delineating our responsibilities. Workplace conflicts rarely occurred. There was great joy associated with working together to bring in new business. While we sometimes wondered if it was a good idea for both of our incomes to be dependent on the same company, we had every confidence that we would be able to keep growing the agency. Thankfully, we were successful, so we had the additional joy of watching the agency prosper.

The biggest challenge was the fact that it was very difficult to turn the business off at the end of the work day. Still, we were generally able to maintain a fairly healthy balance – even if our young daughter would often proclaim at dinner, "Could you please stop talking about work?!" Working together at Directech proved to us that it was indeed possible to be a happily married couple and business colleagues as well. It laid the groundwork for something we had never anticipated – starting and running a service business together. And that's the rest of the story.

CHAPTER 1

Owning a Service Business Together

O wning a service business together is exciting, exhilarating and challenging. It creates a whole new dynamic in your relationship.

- We had the advantage of working together at two different companies before we started a business as a couple. In fact, we were business colleagues before we got married. This gave us the opportunity to understand each other's strengths and weaknesses and learn how to blend our styles to work together.

- Compatibility as a couple is not the same thing as compatibility as business owners. Some couples love each other but could never work together. Be honest with yourselves about whether you are "business compatible." Understand the additional pressure working together can put on your relationship.

- Keep your working relationship professional, especially when you are dealing with employees or clients. Exposing others to your personal lives could make them feel uncomfortable or embarrassed. Never let an employee get caught in the middle of a couple's disagreement.

- If you share a common passion and build your service business around it, you will find it much easier to work together. Working with a common vision and purpose helps you overcome potential conflict in the way you run the business.

Owning a service business together was a natural progression for us rather than a pre-meditated plan. We had already worked together at two different companies. But then two events occurred that laid the foundation for starting a business of our own.

First, Sharon decided she wanted to make a career change. She was tired of her professional career in marketing and sales. She took some time off to consider her next move and realized that what she really wanted to do was work with dogs. She had loved dogs all her life. We both had dogs as kids and we owned dogs throughout our marriage. Sharon explored a number of possible career paths and felt most comfortable with dog grooming. She was drawn to the idea of making dogs feel and look good. Sharon apprenticed at a retail dog grooming salon and enjoyed it so much that she enrolled in dog grooming school.

Barry was going through some changes of his own. Directech, the direct marketing agency he founded, had grown into a well-respected $5 million profitable business, and it was now approaching its twentieth anniversary. Barry and his partner had started to discuss an exit strategy, but they didn't have to think about it for very long. In 2003, with little warning, one of the agency's two biggest clients filed for bankruptcy, leaving Directech with receivables it was unable to collect. Rather than put all of the employees out of work, Barry and his partner were able to strike an agree-

LET'S MAKE MONEY, HONEY • 19

ment with a large Boston ad agency to hire half of the agency's employees, including Barry, and add Directech's other large client to its roster.

RELOCATE AND REWIRE

We didn't realize at the time that these two events – Sharon beginning a new career and Barry leaving the agency he founded – would intersect and be the catalyst for starting a new life as well as starting a new business together. Our daughter would soon be going off to college and we both felt a yearning to make a bold change. We wanted to live somewhere different and do something different. While we loved the Boston area, we were getting tired of the cold, snowy winters and the high cost of living. Barry was now commuting into the city from a suburb west of Boston and it was a real drag. Sharon was working as a groomer for a kennel but wanted more flexibility in her schedule. We were boomers in our fifties looking for the opportunity to rewire our careers and our lives. We worked out a plan with our financial adviser so that making such a major move would be feasible.

The "somewhere different" turned out to be Asheville, North Carolina. We had visited this small city in Western North Carolina several times and thought it would be a great place to live, so that's where we decided to relocate. The "something different" was less obvious. Sharon enjoyed dog grooming, but she wanted to regain her independence instead of working for someone else. Barry wanted to leave the ad agency business and work as a freelance writer part-time, but he also had the entrepreneurial bug. That's when we said to each other, "Let's make money, honey...in a business together."

Since we had worked together for years in a service business, we knew we had complementary skills, and we both felt comfortable building a business around service. With our combined marketing and sales experience, we knew we could do a great job promoting the business. But what would the business be? We thought about various possibilities, but nothing seemed to click. Then we realized there was a potential business idea staring us in the face: Why not build a service business around Sharon's dog grooming abilities?

By this time, Sharon had graduated from grooming school and had been grooming dogs for about five years. She had developed a real talent for it. It was her creative outlet, much the same way Barry's creative outlet was writing.

We wondered if there was a market for dog grooming in Asheville. While we were having a house built there, we began to explore Asheville from a dog owner's perspective (we had two of our own) and quickly realized that it was a very dog-friendly city. In fact, dogs seemed to be everywhere. We saw dogs being walked on city streets, lying beside their owners in restaurant outdoor seating areas, frolicking in dog parks, running with mountain bikers, and hiking with their owners in Bent Creek National Forest and along the Blue Ridge Parkway. There were plenty of businesses servicing dogs and their owners: pet stores, kennels, dog sitters, dog walkers, dog bakeries, dog boutiques, veterinarians, and groomers.

BARKING UP THE RIGHT TREE

We were convinced there were enough dogs to warrant another dog groomer, but instead of starting from scratch, we thought it might be smarter to acquire an on-going operation so we could get up to speed quickly and at minimum risk. Even before relocating, we came up with a "business acquisition process" that included the following steps:

1. Research dog groomers in the Asheville area and map their locations to determine their service areas
2. Conduct drive-bys to assess the appearance of select businesses based on their location
3. Compose and send a personal letter to those grooming businesses we might have an interest in acquiring
4. Create a Confidentiality Agreement to be signed by prospective sellers
5. Based on response to the letter, meet with prospective sellers
6. Evaluate the business on the following criteria:
    a. Service area and competition
    b. Income for 3 years
    c. Number of customers and customer turnover
    d. Types of grooms and prices charged
    e. Reputation
    f. Business growth potential
    g. Assets, equipment and location
    h. Expenses
    i. Employees
    j. Exit plan of owner
7. Negotiate with appropriate seller
8. Obtain financing
9. Purchase business and "re-open" it under our ownership

The letter we sent over Sharon's signature read, in part:

I would like to take over an existing grooming business with an established clientele. I have no idea if you have ever thought about selling your business, but if there is a chance you might consider it, I would like to speak with you. If you have a potential interest, I can be flexible. For example, I would be happy to have you continue to work in the business, if you so desire.

We didn't know if anyone would have an interest in selling their grooming business. We were delighted to get responses from two business owners. We sketched out the questions we wanted to ask them, drafted a confidentiality agreement for them to sign, and made arrangements to meet them.

The two businesses were very different. One groomer was located in a town south of Asheville and had been open for only a short time. The owners, also a wife and husband, were interested in selling because they planned to relocate elsewhere. The other business was right in Asheville, had been operating for quite a while, and had an established reputation. The owner/groomer was interested in retiring from the business. We did our due diligence and evaluated both of them using the criteria we had established.

When we returned home, we pored over the information we had obtained and reviewed the photos we had taken of each operation. As we discussed the pros and cons, we realized something about both dog grooming businesses: It dawned on us that they were *retail operations*. These groomers had to keep their shops open all day, every day, just like a retail store. While their businesses primarily consisted of customers who made appointments to have their dogs groomed, anyone could walk in during the day to buy merchandise or make an appointment. If the groomers weren't busy, they would even agree to groom walk-ins, not unlike a beauty salon that accepts walk-in customers for hair styling.

We wrestled with the idea of running a full-time retail business. While Sharon loved the idea of grooming dogs and being her own boss, she didn't like the idea of working retail hours or paying monthly rent. In fact, neither of us could justify the time commitment we felt would be needed to operate a retail store. We really didn't want to be held prisoner by a business that needed to be opened five or even six days a week, eight or nine hours a day. It would likely mean that Sharon would have to work full-time, which wasn't her interest, and it very well could mean hiring other employees. We didn't want that either – we knew from past experience that personnel management was a challenge we'd rather avoid.

We were in a quandary. We believed both of the grooming businesses had potential. We thought the owners would be willing to sell if we offered a fair price. The problem was now we were anything but sure that we wanted to run a retail dog grooming business. We weren't afraid of working hard to open and build a business, but we just couldn't get used to the idea of being full-time retailers. So where would we go from here?

THE "AHA!" MOMENT

Discouraged but not deterred, we thought about alternatives to running a traditional retail store. For example, we considered operating a grooming parlor with hours by appointment only and no merchandise component, which would limit the time we would have to be open. We dismissed that idea, because we figured it would be an inefficient use of rented space and our operating costs would be too high.

Then one day, Sharon was looking through a grooming magazine and she read an article about mobile dog grooming. Apparently, there was an entire segment of the grooming industry that was literally on wheels. Mobile groomers in specially equipped vans went to customers' homes to groom their dogs. It appeared that this service was especially popular in Florida and California.

We talked about the mobile dog grooming concept and found it immediately appealing. With a mobile grooming van, Sharon could be her own boss and we could run our own business without the constraints of a retail store. Sharon could set her own schedule and work as little or as much as she wanted, so she would have maximum flexibility. With Barry handling the business and marketing, Sharon could concentrate on grooming and not have to worry about the business details.

The more we thought about it, the more we thought mobile dog grooming would be perfectly suited to Asheville. Here's why: When we were exploring Asheville's housing market, we noticed that the nicest homes were located in residential communities. Unlike where we lived in Massachusetts, the Asheville area had no zoning to protect residential neighborhoods. If you didn't live in a residential community, you had the potential of having an industrial plant as your neighbor. That's right, just about anything could be built right next door to your home. This was the reason we bought a home in a South Asheville residential community, and why communities were so popular in the Asheville area.

Because residential communities were common, they made easy targets for mobile dog grooming. We reasoned that if we could target our business and saturate certain communities close to one other, we could keep travel to a minimum. That would limit our gas usage, which we assumed was going to be a big expense of mobile grooming. As we researched the business further, it became clear that mobile dog groomers were charging higher prices than retail grooming operations. As a result customers would self-select; a customer had to be able to want and afford the convenience of mobile grooming. Clearly, it was a service designed for upscale dog owners who were not going to object to paying a premium price.

Mobile dog grooming was our "Aha!" moment. We politely told the owners of the two grooming businesses we had been considering that we were no longer able to pursue a possible acquisition. Instead, we began to conceptualize plans for a mobile dog grooming business. We found out there were a few other mobile dog groomers operating in the Asheville area, but we felt there would be plenty of business for us.

Sharon already had a name in mind: Bandanas. I liked it right away – Asheville was located in Western North Carolina, which had its own rugged, individual connotation. No, it wasn't "cowboy country," but we did see lots of dogs in Asheville wearing bandanas. We also knew it was common for dog groomers to give out bandanas with each groom. The name was relevant and had a friendly sound. I suggested calling the service "Bandanas Mobile Grooming Salon." And so a business idea was born.

WHAT'S *YOUR* "AHA!" MOMENT?

Let's face it – dog grooming isn't for everyone. But it seemed like a great fit for us, given Sharon's skill and passion, Barry's desire to try his hand at something new and different, and what we both perceived was a business opportunity with real potential. It was a service business that would involve dealing directly with clients, and given our background, we were comfortable with that.

Luckily for us, it turned out that pet services was a booming segment of the service industry, and it still is. If you both love pets, there are other opportunities in this area that may be of interest to you, including dog walking, pet sitting, and even removing dog poop; in fact, we know a local entrepreneur who is cleaning up...!

Obviously, one of the biggest decisions you'll have to make early on is what type of service business you both want to start and run. We believe strongly that a couple needs to have a common passion that turns into a common vision for a business. This doesn't mean you both have to be passionate about the same thing, but it does mean you have to share the same goal. In our case, Sharon was passionate about dog grooming, and Barry was passionate about running a service business. She had the specific skill set for the particular service; he had the ability to apply his broad business management and marketing experience to starting and running the business. Barry just as easily could have started another type of service business, but he recognized he could be a good partner and contribute to a business that centered around Sharon's skills. We both had a passion for animals and also for providing excellent service to clients.

As you think about the type of service business you might want to operate, take a critical look at your strengths and weaknesses, as well as your interests. What are you both passionate about? Is there something that each of you love to do that has the potential to cross over? Can you leverage your past business experience to create a new business opportunity for both of you? The key thing is to find common ground and a common sense of purpose. Sound familiar? It should – the process of deciding on what business to pursue isn't too different from understanding how to make life decisions together as a couple.

It makes sense before you decide on a particular business to research service business ideas that have the greatest potential. Countless service businesses exist in a wide variety of areas. These businesses are generally divided into two categories: services to consumers and services to businesses. These categories are further sub-divided based on the type of services provided. You'll be able to make some obvious initial cuts; for example, if neither you nor your partner are particularly interested in financial management, you certainly wouldn't want to start a business that offers bookkeeping or accounting services. If either of you has experience in past positions working with businesses, you might be comfortable starting a business that focuses on servicing businesses rather than consumers.

There are many lists of top service business ideas. Sources worth exploring include the magazines *Entrepreneur, Fast Company,* and *Inc.,* the newspaper *The Wall Street Journal,* and government sources such as the Small Business Administration (www.sba.gov) and the Bureau of Labor Statistics (www.bls.gov). Additional sources are listed in the **Resources** section of this book.

When you are deciding on a service business, you need to look at a combination of factors to minimize your risk. Your decision should include not only your skills and interests but also the potential need for the services you wish to provide in your particular geographic or trading area. If you want to run a service business near where you live, do some research to determine whether there is enough revenue potential in your area and what competition may exist for your particular kind of business. If your idea involves running an online service business, your geographic area may be less relevant, but the online competitive environment becomes all the more important.

Look at the process as a kind of balancing act: Balance your capabilities and your business interests against the potential for success in the service area you select. On the positive side, if you both have years of experience working for other companies, you are well aware of your capabilities as individuals. You probably already have a good amount of business acumen. If your experience includes dealing directly with customers or clients, so much the better. Having previous experience working in the business world will significantly limit your risk – and this is one reason why starting a service business together is ideally suited to more mature couples.

So what is the best way to evaluate a business idea and turn it into a reality? That's what we'll talk about in the next chapter.

Consider This...

- Think long and hard about owning a business together before you make the move.
- Be honest with yourselves about your desire and ability to work together.
- Understand and appreciate your differences and turn them into complementary assets instead of liabilities.

We were fortunate in that we had worked together at two different companies before starting our own business together. Because of these previous experiences, we got to know each other's working style, each other's strengths and weaknesses, and how we could best complement each other's capabilities. We learned, for example, that Barry was more conceptual – the "big idea" person – with a penchant for creative writing. Sharon was more pragmatic, the down-to-the-details person. But we were both hell-bent on quality and service. This made for a great team, since our skill sets were different but our values were the same. Still, Sharon could contribute ideas and Barry could relate to things at the detail level. We respected and were accepting of each other's capabilities. Our personalities were also different yet complementary – Barry tended to be "hot" – a little more intense – while Sharon was "cool" – level-headed and steady. You might say the sum of the parts was greater than the whole.

You and your partner should do a self-assessment (we've included an assessment tool in Chapter 9) so you can identify your unique skills and learn how you both can make the best use of your talents and capabilities without conflicting with one another. For couples to be successful at working together, they need to understand and acknowledge each other's differences, define distinct roles, treat each other with mutual respect, and be willing to share power. In fact, throughout our business and personal lives, we have each made an effort to "pass the power ball" back and forth, always making sure that one person is never calling all the shots all the time.

Here's something else you may have to work on: Living together and working together as a couple can be intense and, at times, overwhelming. As we learned even before we owned a business, working together blends a couple's personal lives with their careers, and it's very difficult to maintain separation between these two aspects of life. It's only natural to discuss business situations that you face even when you are out of the office. You need to remember, however, that setting boundaries is important to the health of yourselves and other members of your family. Just like sharing power, knowing when to turn off your business life and protect your personal life is an acquired skill that takes some practice.

As you're considering co-owning a business, ask yourselves the following questions:

1. Are we starting a business we both share a passion about – a business built on common ground that both of us can embrace and enjoy?

2. Are we in a financial position, or do we have access to financing, that allows us to start a business without putting our personal lives at risk?

3. Is my partner someone I think I could work with in a business setting, day in and day out, sharing the pressures and challenges of running a business?

4. Can we maintain a professional distance from each other and work as business partners without letting personal issues get in the way?

5. Do we have complementary skills that will allow each of us to play specific and distinct roles, making the business stronger because of our combined skills, and are we able to blend these skills together without causing conflict?

6. Are we willing to share the responsibility of owning a business together, understanding that our personal and business lives will overlap and it is often difficult to separate the two?

7. Do we have the type of relationship in which we can "pass the power ball" back and forth so both partners feel equally empowered?

CHAPTER 2

Planning the Business

P lanning your business is essential. Planning may not *guarantee* your success, but it will greatly improve your chances of success.

- Write a business plan, even if you don't think you will need investment capital. A business plan isn't just for investors, it is a blueprint for success. A business plan is valuable because it makes you flesh out a business idea and work through the necessary steps to turn it into a viable business.

- Consider all your options before you start your own service business, including buying an existing business or buying a franchise.

- A key reason new businesses fail is because they are under-capitalized. Make sure you over-estimate startup and annual expenses and under-estimate income. You should have enough capital available to sustain your business for at least one year.

- Self-funding a business is the most common way to start a service business. However, if using your own capital puts your family, your home, or your personal life at risk, it is better to seek outside loans or investors.

We had our business idea – mobile dog grooming – and our business name: Bandanas Mobile Grooming Salon. Now what?

Barry knew from starting his direct marketing agency almost twenty-five years ago that a business concept and a name were nice to have, but it took a lot more than that to start a business. He felt it would be necessary to go through what has become a standard process for starting up a business: Writing a business plan.

THE BUSINESS PLAN

Most small business owners seem to approach writing a business plan much the same way they would approach a visit to the dentist: They know they really need to do it, but it isn't something they look forward to. Honestly, it wasn't much different for us. We were planning to self-fund our business, so we didn't need a business plan to submit to potential investors, which is one of the primary reasons to create a business plan. Still, a business plan is just as important for a business owner who wants to flesh out an idea and turn it into a viable business, even if startup capital is not required. A well thought out business plan provides a solid foundation for the business so that it has the best chance to succeed.

The content of a business plan may vary, but every business plan covers the same basic territory. Most business plans include:

Executive Summary

The Executive Summary should succinctly present an overview of the business and its reason for being, including the business objectives and how the company hopes to achieve them. Particularly important is the problem the business hopes to solve or the market need it hopes to fill. To some extent, this section summarizes the entire business plan, but only at a high level. The Executive Summary also typically includes the company's philosophy, often presented in the form of a "mission statement." A well-written Executive Summary supported by smart thinking and facts can get an investor interested in a business.

Business Description

This section describes in detail the nature of the business; the legal organization (type of business entity, such as proprietorship, LLC, etc.); company management; business attributes such as location, services provided, and staff; and the functional areas of the company, including finance, human resources, marketing, and customer service.

Marketing and Sales

Every business needs to have an in-depth understanding of its market, for without a viable market, there can be no sustainable business. This section needs to present market research and analysis that validates the existence of the market for the business. It typically also includes a discussion of items generally classified under the "Marketing" umbrella: audience characteristics; competitors and competitive analysis; pricing strategy; business and brand attributes and benefits; marketing strategy, including references to forms of advertising and promotion that will be used to support the business. A discussion of sales strategy should also be included.

Financial

The Financial section should include everything an investor would want to know about the financial operation of the business. Typically, this section includes startup expenses; available startup capital vs. investment capital required; sales forecast for at least one year; projected income and expenses, at least for the first year, but often for at least three years; and various financial reports that investors would expect, including profit and loss, balance sheet, a cash flow projection, and break-even analysis.

There are numerous sources (books, CDs, and websites) with instructions for how to write a business plan, template business plans, and sample financial spreadsheets. Some sources are listed in the Resources section of this guide. You will also find a sample business plan for a service business at the end of this guide.

With all the sources available, there really is no reason a small business owner has to reinvent the wheel. You should be sure, however, to select a source that accommodates a service business. While you could adapt a product-focused business plan to your needs, it is easier to work with templates and forms designed for a service business. Read product reviews and customer comments and purchase a product that seems comprehensive yet easy to use. You will probably find that available tools often include more than you will ever need, so try to avoid paying for bells and whistles you won't use.

We purchased a simple software program that provided guidance on what to write in each section. It also included templates of uncomplicated financial spreadsheets that could be run in Microsoft Excel. These were very helpful in allowing us to run various income and expense projections. One thing we quickly learned about the program we used – and we're quite sure this would be true of any program. The book, CD or website you use to create a business plan is a tool and nothing more. It helps you to know what should be included in a business plan, and it can make it easier to formulate a budget. But the ideas for your business, the description of your marketing strategy, and the financial spreadsheets that show expenses, income and profit come from one place: **you.** You still have to do the work!

While we weren't seeking startup capital, we found that the business plan was essential to us for these other reasons:

1. We were able to plan what type of business organization we wanted to have
2. We could carefully research the market for our service business
3. Once we decided that mobile dog grooming was the way to go, the plan led us to research the options available for equipping a mobile dog grooming operation
4. We could estimate our startup costs
5. We were able to run several projections of income vs. expenses for a typical year so we would know how many grooms per day Sharon would need to do and how many days per week she would have to work to cover our expenses and make a profit.

Writing a good business plan takes a fair amount of skill and a commitment of time. It is a combination of excellent strategic thinking, strong descriptive copy, and accurate financial information.

OUR OWN BUSINESS... OR A FRANCHISE?

One of the possible avenues we considered was a franchise. Franchises are a way to enter a business using a proven business system created by someone else. The franchisor typically provides the product or the service and offers full business and marketing support to the franchisee. In some cases, the franchisor also helps secure the appropriate location for the franchisee's business. In return, the franchisee pays a startup fee and a percentage of the sales of the franchise. While franchises are more common for retail product operations, they do exist for service businesses.

During our research into mobile dog grooming, we ran across a few franchise operations, the largest of which was a company called Aussie Pet Mobile. While Aussie had started in Australia, it aggressively expanded globally and had more than 500 territories in the United States. The benefits of a franchise such as Aussie is that the franchisor provides a specially outfitted dog grooming vehicle under its own name, as well as groomer training, a business system, and marketing support. In effect, the franchisor offers a complete system. The franchisee has to pay a startup fee as well as a percentage of sales to participate in the system.

While there were elements of franchising that we found attractive, we decided against the franchise model. Sharon was already an experienced groomer and didn't require training. Barry was knowledgeable about starting and running a service business. Both of us had considerable experience in marketing and sales. We felt there would be no real advantage investing our money in a franchise and paying someone else for equipment, business guidance and marketing support when we were confident we could do it on our own. We also wanted to maintain our independence, be our own boss, and make sure that Sharon did not have the pressure of having to achieve a certain level of income determined by the franchisor.

Despite our decision to start and operate the business ourselves, there are times when a franchise might be an attractive option for a couple starting a service business. A franchise could be a good choice if you are not very familiar with the type of service you will be offering, if you do not have a strong business background, or if you do not have the marketing and sales experience necessary to make the business successful. Certain service businesses are well-suited for franchising, and it is very possible that a franchise may exist for a business you would like to run. It probably makes sense to at least consider the franchise option, as we did, to determine if it is an alternative worth pursuing.

FUNDING OPTIONS

Many new businesses fail for one key reason: lack of sufficient funding. Once you complete your business plan, you should have a good idea of the startup costs for your business. Here's a piece of advice: Figure out your startup costs and then add a contingency of at least 20 to 30 percent. Even if you accurately estimate your startup costs, it is always a good idea to plan for the unexpected – and that's what the contingency is for.

Also, keep in mind that the term "startup" is somewhat of a misnomer. The costs to start up a service business may look fairly reasonable to begin with – after all, most service businesses don't need an inventory of products to sell. However, your true startup costs should include what it would cost for you to operate for at least a year, using a very conservative income estimate. Unlike a business that sells products, a service business could take longer to generate income, even though your costs might be less because you are not buying or manufacturing products. Usually, purchasing a service costs more than purchasing a product, and since a service is less defined than a product, it could be a more difficult sale to make. A service business tends to rely on reputation and referrals, so it may take months before you make your first sale.

Your business plan should include a budget that over-estimates your startup costs and under-estimates your income so you protect yourself from unrealistic expectations. This puts you in a position to have a better understanding of what kind of capital you will need to not just start your business, but to sustain it through the first year. If you are seeking funding from an outside source, it is always a good idea to have more than one scenario for income and expenses. At least one scenario should show a projected profit in the first year, after accounting for startup costs. You want to show a potential investor that your business idea is viable and that you have the right elements in place to make it happen.

With this in mind, it's time to think about funding options. The old saying, "You need money to make money" applies in this case. Capital for a new service business typically comes from one or more of the following sources:

1. **Self-funding**

Self-funding is the most common way to start a service business. This type of funding is exactly what it sounds like: You fund the business with your own money. That's how we started Bandanas Mobile Grooming Salon. We sold our house in Massachusetts for a substantial enough price that we were able to take a portion of the proceeds to start up our business. We had an advantage in that we sold our house when real estate prices were at their peak. After the sale, we were left with enough equity available to apply to starting a business. Everything worked out well for us.

On the other hand, we wouldn't necessarily recommend selling your house at the same time as starting a business!

You may have investments, savings, real estate holdings, or other sources of income with which you could fund your business. Just be sure you have sufficient capital for the business without putting your personal life at risk. There is always some risk involved, of course, but it is a matter of degree. For example, you might be able to use an equity line on your current home to start a business, but you need to be confident you can eventually pay it off. Putting your home at risk to start your business isn't the ideal strategy to pursue.

2. **Banks**

Banks are a natural avenue for seeking funding, but in recent years, bank credit has tightened up significantly, making it more difficult to get a business loan. Still, a regional or local community bank or credit union should be high on your list of potential funding sources. The bank may be a lender authorized to make SBA loans as well (see Government loans, below.) It pays to build a relationship with a bank branch manager or someone at the branch who works with small businesses. Express an interest in opening a business checking account, getting a business credit card, and potentially using the bank's merchant credit card services if you wish to accept credit card payments from customers. At the same time, find out if the bank is making business loans or extending lines of credit to small businesses.

A loan is different from a line of credit. Typically, a loan is offered at a specific interest rate with a fixed time period to pay it back, not unlike a mortgage on a house. The bank will likely want to see financials, if not a full business plan. A line of credit is usually extended on a revolving basis, which means you can use the line whenever you need it. You then pay off the amount you used over several months, in effect, rebuilding the credit line. Credit lines are usually used to ease temporary cash flow problems rather than start businesses. Whether you are able to obtain a loan or secure a credit line, be sure you understand the terms, the interest, and any penalties associated with late payment or default.

It is not be unusual for you to be asked by a bank to "sign personally" on a loan or a line of credit. This means you personally guarantee that the loan will be paid back. Accepting this responsibility is a risk, but certainly not as big a risk as taking a second mortgage on your house, maxing out a credit card, or cleaning out a savings account to start a business.

3. Angel Investors

"Angel investor" is a term often used to identify an individual investor, rather than an investment firm, such as a venture capitalist firm. An angel investor can be anyone – a relative, friend or neighbor of yours, a former boss or business colleague, a former university professor, someone you meet at a business function or networking event, or even someone you don't personally know. The challenge with angel investors is identifying who they are, since they are not necessarily aligned with any type of investment firm, and they usually don't advertise themselves to the public.

Generally, it makes the most sense to try and find angel investors in your immediate vicinity. Local angel investors would tend to be interested in making an investment in a local company, since it supports their local economy. It is always easier for an angel investor to invest in a company in close proximity, although it is not a pre-requisite. To find local angel investors, you have to think about where they might congregate or what organization they might affiliate with. Local angel investors could themselves be owners or CEOs of local companies, or on the boards of directors of one or more companies. They could be prominent members of the community – lawyers, accountants, or doctors, for example. They could be members of civic organizations, the local Chamber of Commerce, or other local and regional economic development organizations. They may be associated with a local college or university that has an entrepreneurial program or any kind of program that caters to the business community. In rare cases, angel investors form their own associations, groups or clubs. Leave no stone unturned in seeking out angel investors.

Once you identify potential angel investors, your primary objective is to obtain a personal meeting so you can make your pitch, which most often involves giving a presentation and submitting your business plan in person. An angel investor who likes your business plan may want to invest in your business – but it may very well mean that you have to give up a portion of the ownership of your company. This is a difficult decision that only you can make.

4. Government Loans

The best-known source of government loans for small business is the federal government's Small Business Administration (SBA). The SBA offers a number of different loan programs, based on type of business and determination of need. Many of these loan programs are administered by banks or authorized nonprofit organizations involved in community and economic development. The SBA's website (www.sba.gov) has comprehensive information about its loan programs.

While the SBA is the proverbial "big gorilla" when it comes to government-sponsored small business loans, it could be well worth your while to do additional research into government loans that may be available through other federal agencies, or via small business-related government agencies in your city, county, region or state. Local governments recognize that small businesses fuel the economy and they may have loan programs available that could be sources of funding to start your business.

5. Non-Government Loans and Grants

Several other organizations exist outside the context of government that may offer loans, grants, and awards available to startup businesses. Search for nonprofit organizations, foundations, and economic/community development organizations whose mission is to facilitate business growth. Sometimes, a professional association that serves your industry might make small funding programs available to startup businesses. While each of these organizations will have different requirements, application forms, and deadline dates, they are all viable sources of funding.

6. Business Incubators

Business incubators are structures typically established by community colleges or universities with the purpose of literally incubating new businesses. They do this by offering startups the opportunity to rent office space at below-market rates, share resources such as meeting rooms, telephone systems, computers, and copiers, and receive business guidance and counseling. Typically, a business owner must make an application and submit a business plan in order to qualify for acceptance into a business incubator. Some incubators also make small grants or awards to help these businesses get started and grow. While a business incubator is not in the business of making direct business loans, its in-kind services can be just as valuable as money to startup businesses accepted into their program.

7. Microlending

Microlending has been fueled by an online phenomenon often referred to as crowdsourcing or crowdfunding. In microlending, a business entrepreneur basically makes a pitch for money online, through a microlending site, to fund a project. While there are several such sites (see the *Resources* section at the end of this book), one of the leaders is Kickstarter.com. With Kickstarter, an individual asks for funding for a specific project, as opposed to a business. Anyone can participate in funding the project, as long as they meet the minimum funding amount. This is how Kickstarter explains its project funding on its website:

"Every project creator sets their project's funding goal and deadline. If people like the project, they can pledge money to make it happen. If the project succeeds in reaching its funding goal, all backers' credit cards are charged when time expires. If the project falls short, no one is charged. Funding on Kickstarter is all-or-nothing."

Microlending is a very specialized form of funding. In generally, it is more appropriate for funding projects and companies with specific products to sell; however, it may be possible to use microlending to fund a service business as well.

Consider This...

We had an idea for a business in an area we were both passionate about (dogs), and we also had the right combination of skills. Sharon was an experienced dog groomer who had previously been in marketing and sales. This is unusual – most dog groomers have little or no marketing or sales experience. As a result, Sharon both understood the marketing/sales process and had great customer service skills. Barry had operated his own service business and had a strong background in marketing. This meant he could manage and market the business and leave Sharon free to do grooming. Together, we forged a strong team with complementary skills, increasing our chance for success.

When you are considering what type of service business to start together, **find something you are both passionate about.** Then evaluate your individual skill sets. (Use the "Skills Inventory Checklist" in Chapter 9.) Start a business that takes advantage of your skills, one in which you can collaborate, cooperate, and contribute equally. It is important to be a coordinated team from the very beginning.

While both of you should have input into the business plan, one of you should take the lead when it comes to writing it. It is important for the plan to have a "single voice." If you will be seeking outside funding to start your business, it is likely that your business plan will need to be more comprehensive and detailed than if you are self-funding your business. Even if you self-fund, however, go through the exercise of creating a business plan. The business plan process will help you validate your business approach and ensure that there is an adequate market for your business. Working through the financial requirements of a business plan will be extremely valuable in helping you determine your startup costs and forecast your income and expenses. Accurate income, expense and cash flow projections can make the difference between success and failure.

Carefully consider how you should fund your business. Self-funding is obviously attractive because you are not dependent on anyone but yourselves, but be sure you are not putting your personal lives at risk. If you want to self-fund your business, you should have enough capital available to cover your startup costs and at least the first year of business operation. Use conservative projections: Over-estimate your expenses and under-estimate your income for the first year. It's always better to have a good surprise than a bad one.

If you decide to seek outside capital to start your business, research all potential funding sources available – banks, angel investors, government agencies, other organizations and foundations, business incubators, and microlenders. Evaluate each one and compare what they can offer you. While the interest you pay on a loan is obviously an important factor, your decision to use one source over another should also be based on the relationship you could potentially build with the lender. For example, the lender might be able to refer business to you, or put you in touch with resources you would find valuable. In the end, it might be worth paying a slightly higher interest rate to a lender who can offer you something extra that may help you succeed.

When you apply for any kind of funding, be fully prepared:

1. Create an *elevator pitch* for your business. This is a succinct statement that describes the vision and goals for your business. It should take no more than two minutes to deliver. Write it out and practice it on each other, on rela-

tives and friends, and at business meetings. Refine it until you are happy with it.

2. Have a completed business plan available. Some lenders will ask for additional information about your personal finances, since you are both principals of the business.

3. If you plan to ask for capital from an angel investor, it is important to find out what the investor needs from you to make an informed decision. Depending on the investor, you may need to complete an application, submit a written document, and make a presentation. If a presentation is required, determine how much time you will be given and what format is preferred by the investor. In most cases, a presentation will need to include slides that excerpt the highlights of your business plan.

4. Be courteous and professional when dealing with any potential investors or lenders. First impressions are lasting, and the way you both present yourselves can make a difference in the lending or investing outcome.

CHAPTER 3

Outfitting the Business

Y our business plan is your security blanket, giving you the confidence you need to take the next step. Now you can begin executing that plan by establishing and outfitting your business.

- Proceed in a logical sequence. Establish your business name (and be sure it isn't already taken). Discuss who will own the business. Then determine what form your business will take. You will need to decide whether your business will be a non-incorporated proprietorship, a partnership, or a corporation. There are plusses and minuses to each business type.

- Understand the legal requirements associated with establishing a business in your area. Most cities or counties require new businesses to file some sort of document. Depending on the form your business takes, states and the Federal government have different filing requirements.

- Form a relationship with a bank and open a business checking account. Find out what other business services the bank can offer you, such as merchant credit card services, a business credit card, a business line of credit, and business loans.

- Using the startup costs you projected as a budget, locate a suitable space for your business and outfit your business with the necessary equipment.

We had a business name we were happy with, a business plan that suggested there was a market for our service, and our own "seed money" to start the business. Now it was time to get serious.

The first thing we did was evaluate the various legal forms our business could take. We agreed that it would be most advantageous and less complicated if Sharon were to be the sole owner of the business. Barry already owned his own writing and consulting business, and while he would be actively involved in helping Sharon operate Bandanas, he did not feel being co-owner of the business held any advantage.

Determining who owns your business is a very personal decision, but it is important to establish ownership upfront. If you each decide you would like to participate in owning the business equally, there is nothing wrong with that, as long as you both recognize that business ownership has specific responsibilities. Being a business owner means you are directly responsible for business operations, profit, paying taxes, filing legal documents, and employing people, if that should become necessary.

Co-owning a business, even under the best of circumstances, is always a challenge. Co-owning a business means you have to be able to agree on business goals and business decisions. This may seem like a great idea as you're starting a business, but it could backfire later. For example, Barry remembers that when he first started his direct marketing agency, he ran it as a sole proprietorship. As the agency grew, however, he wanted to bring others into the business. One person in particular seemed like she would be the perfect partner, so he agreed to form a corporation with himself and his partner as co-owners. They each agreed to own 50 percent of the corporation.

Years later, when Barry and his partner began to diverge on the way they thought the business should be managed, it became very difficult to resolve their differences. As equal partners, neither individual had the majority right to control the business. At one point, Barry even thought about leaving the agency he had founded and starting another business. A legal dispute ensued and, eventually, an agreement was reached for Barry to buy out his partner's interest in the agency. The process was wrought with emotion and it distracted Barry from running the business. Barry never again took on a co-equal partner; in fact, his early experience with partnerships may have been one of the reasons he did not want to co-own Bandanas with Sharon.

As a couple, you may think splitting a business equally down the middle is the best strategy. For some couples, this works just fine. But if there is ever a dispute or serious disagreement, co-equal ownership might make it difficult if not impossible to resolve the issue. Not only could co-ownership turn into a messy business break-up, it could also lead to relationship problems for a couple. Sadly, stories about family businesses that have been torn to shreds by couples who no longer see eye to eye are quite common.

You would be wise to discuss with each other what business ownership really means in an open, honest way. It is also a good idea to get the advice of legal counsel and an accountant before you decide on the ownership and legal structure of your business.

FORMING AN LLC
After discussing the pros and cons of potential forms our business could take, we decided on a Limited Liability Corporation (LLC).

While some states require at least two individuals to form an LLC, a North Carolina LLC could be established with a single person, so we formed "Bandanas Mobile Grooming Salon LLC" with Sharon as the sole member/owner (that is the terminology used in defining the ownership of an LLC). Forming the LLC was as simple as ensuring that the name was available and filing a standard "articles of organization" document with the Secretary of State of North Carolina. The only additional expense involved was the North Carolina requirement to file an annual report for the business (just a formality) at a cost of $200 each year.

As attorney Daniel Sitarz points out in his book, *Limited Liability Company Small Business Start-Up Kit*, there are a number of advantages to the LLC, which is essentially a cross between a partnership and a corporation:

> *In general, the member's risk is limited to the amount of their investment in the limited liability company. ...Since the limited liability company is generally taxed as a partnership, the profits and losses of the company pass directly to each member and are taxed only at the individual level. ... A further advantage of this type of business structure is that it offers a relatively flexible management structure. The company can be managed either by members (owners) themselves or by managers who may or may not be members. ...A final advantage is that limited liability companies are allowed more flexibility than corporations in how profits and losses are actually allocated to the members/owners.*[3]

Daniel Sitarz does a thorough job of laying out the disadvantages and advantages of each type of business structure – sole proprietorship, partnership, and various forms of corporations (C-Corporation, S-Corporation, and Limited Liability Company). His book offers valuable expert guidance that can prevent the fledgling business owner from selecting the wrong type of business structure. Sitarz goes one step further, providing a comprehensive guide to starting a business, including startup checklists, a model financial plan, tax schedules, state-specific forms, articles of organization, and more.

From a tax accounting perspective, the LLC is advantageous, because documenting the operations of the business is relatively uncomplicated. With an LLC, business expenses and profit/loss can be reported as part of a personal income tax return rather than a corporate income tax return. This both simplifies tax reporting and means that profits are taxed at a generally more favorable personal tax rate. We were able to report the income from the Bandanas LLC on Schedule C of our joint tax return. It is, of course, important to discuss formation of an LLC with an accountant to determine if this business structure is financially beneficial to you.

LOCATING YOUR BUSINESS AND ACQUIRING BUSINESS ASSETS

Unless you run your business out of your home, one of the first things you will have to consider is where to locate your business. An in-home business location may be appropriate in some cases. For example, an online business could start in a garage, basement or a spare room of the owner's home. A small professional consulting business often doesn't need much more than a home-based office. For many new businesses, though, renting office space is a necessity.

In general, the first consideration is picking a location that is convenient for you and for your customers. Include in your budget an amount for office space that is suitable but not overly extravagant. An attractive option for some businesses could be shared office space, in which you pay rent for a small office and the use of common resources, such as a conference room, copier, computer, and even telephone system. Check and see if there are any shared space facilities in your area. Another possibility is sharing space with another small business. You might even be able to partner with a small business to provide capabilities beyond those that you offer. Small business incubators, mentioned in the previous chapter, also offer a new business the potential for very low office rental costs and use of shared resources, as long as the business qualifies.

If you don't have the type of business in which it is necessary for customers to visit, you will have more flexibility in the type of office space you need. Renting rather than purchasing commercial real estate is probably the best option for a new business. Purchasing commercial real estate may offer significant advantages for an established business, but it is generally not a wise financial move for a startup.

Since our business was mobile dog grooming, we did not need to rent office space. The primary business was to be conducted via a specially equipped van (more about that in a moment), so a storefront or commercial business location was unnecessary. Still, there were administrative tasks that needed to be done that we could not perform in the van, so Bandanas shared an office – a separate room in our home – with Barry's business. The two businesses also shared supplies and office equipment, which consisted of a computer and printer, as well as Internet access. We established a separate telephone number, but we did not install a phone line; instead of getting a phone, we restricted the number only to inbound calls so clients could leave messages. Sharon used her cell phone to call in and check messages and to speak with clients. Bandanas also had a website with email access. Email became an important way to communicate with clients. We'll discuss the website and email in a subsequent chapter.

NOW ABOUT THAT VAN...

If you are not familiar with dog grooming, let us give you a quick orientation so that you understand the needs of the business and what it takes to accommodate those needs in a mobile grooming van. Here's the scenario in a typical retail dog grooming salon:

A dog owner calls the grooming salon for an appointment. The owner then brings the dog to the salon at the appointed time. Typically, the owner discusses the type of groom she wants and leaves the dog at the salon for the day, arranging to pick the dog up when the groom is completed.

That's when the fun begins. Behind the scenes, the dog is likely to be one of numerous dogs going through what amounts to a grooming production line. In a grooming salon with multiple groomers, it is not uncommon to groom dogs in stages. Generally, dog grooming involves bathing, drying, nail clipping, brushing, trimming and, if appropriate, getting a haircut with clippers and scissors. Depending on how many dogs the grooming salon needs to handle in a day, these phases might be completed at different times. Dogs could be cycling through the various phases and having to wait in cages between phases. This is why a retail groomer likes the dog to be left for the day.

The equipment involved in dog grooming is substantial. A dog grooming salon needs to have one or more grooming tubs with hot and cold water and special bathing attachments, commercial-quality dryers, grooming tables, and other equipment that may include electric clippers, scissors, combs, brushes, and a "clipper vac" that attaches to a clipper so hair can be vacuumed instead of falling on the floor. Supplies include towels, a variety of shampoos, bandanas, and other consumables.

The reason we are sharing this level of detail with you is to give you some idea of what we needed to include in a mobile grooming van. Essentially, everything we described above needed to be housed on four wheels! The good news is we didn't have to think about how to do that. In fact, we learned that there were several companies that designed custom mobile dog grooming vans. We found all of them online and did a thorough evaluation of what we would need and, also, what we could realistically afford. Once again, our business plan was essential here, because we could plug in the cost of various vans and see the impact on the business. We learned from our accountant that the cost of the van could be amortized over time, but we still had to pay for it upfront.

We wanted a van that was rugged, compact, fuel-efficient and as foolproof as possible to operate. After looking at everything that was available, we decided it was just as important to purchase the right type of van as it was to have a company that would stand behind it. We found a company that specialized in outfitting Sprinter vans with mobile grooming equipment. In a happy coincidence, the company was located less than two hours from Asheville, so we were able to visit there and see exactly what we would be getting. Their convenient location not only made it easy to pick up the van when it was completed, but we were also able to get the van equipment serviced when needed. That turned out to be a major advantage. We relied on the company for regular check-ups and when something went wrong with the grooming systems in the van (which did happen, but not very often), it was great to have the company nearby.

A Sprinter van has a Mercedes diesel engine, so it is extremely efficient. It also has a high yet streamlined profile which makes it very easy to drive. There is enough interior space for a groomer to stand up straight in the back of the van. Since the company specialized in grooming systems, the van was self-contained and outfitted with everything we needed: A hydraulic grooming table with gentle restraints, a grooming tub with hot and cold water and a hydro-massage system, a high velocity multi-speed dryer, a clipper vac (a vacuum that attaches to a clipper and also acts as a vacuum to clean up the hair), and multiple electric outlets. The van was equipped with an "inverter" – a bank of special batteries that had the power to run the equipment without connecting to an exterior power source – along with tanks to carry fresh water and dirty water. The back of the van had its own separate heater and air conditioner, along with roof vents and music speakers. We even had a back-up camera installed. All of this was not just good for the groomer and each dog that was groomed, it was also useful for marketing purposes, because we could actively promote the benefits of mobile dog grooming and the great service that could be provided because of the self-contained van. We could demonstrate that we had the right equipment to do the job in a quality way, grooming one dog at a time.

We could have purchased a used van, but since the van was to be the heart of our business, we purchased a new one. We wanted to own a van and equipment that would last. We also wanted the ability to customize the exterior of the van with our name, logo and phone number, which was easier to do with a new rather than a used van.

We also needed to purchase lots of supplies upfront, such as scissors, clippers, clipper blades, combs, brushes, shampoos, conditioners, bandanas, and more. This type of business was not only dependent on equipment, but also on consumables!

THE SYSTEM IS THE SOLUTION
After acquiring the van that would be the core of the business, we needed a system to help us run the business. These days, special-

ized computer software exists for just about everything, and sure enough, when we searched for a software system for dog grooming, there were several products available. After evaluating all of them, we decided to purchase one that was very easy to use and offered a lot of flexibility. It was designed for small grooming operations with the assumption that a groomer-owner without a lot of computer skills would use it. This system allowed us to set up a record for each client, with standard information such as name, address, phone number, and email, and other helpful information, such as the client's vet. The system also allowed for a separate record for every one of the client's pets. As we would later learn, this was essential, since quite a few clients ended up using Bandanas for more than one dog.

The pet record was extremely detailed. It had data fields for name, breed, gender, age, birth date, weight, characteristics, vaccinations, and other health data, as well as a photo of the dog, if desired. The most important aspect of the pet record was the grooming section. Here, Sharon could record detailed information about the clipper blades and scissors she used on every part of the dog's body, types of shampoos and conditioners used, allergies, and notes about each groom. This information could then be printed as a "groomer worksheet" that Sharon could take with her to the dog's next grooming appointment. This proved to be extremely valuable, not just to remind Sharon how the dog was groomed previously, but also because she had information at her fingertips that was useful in conversations with the client. As we'll discuss later, client service was really key to making Bandanas successful.

We only needed one copy of the grooming software, loaded onto a computer in our home office. We could have had a copy reside on a laptop computer which Sharon kept with her, but we didn't think Sharon would want to spend the time during her grooming day to enter notes into a computer system. We also didn't particularly like the idea of exposing a computer to the hair and moisture associated with a grooming environment. Instead, Sharon brought her groomer worksheets with her for the day and wrote down any necessary notes, transferring them onto each pet's record in the evening. At first, this seemed tedious, but since Sharon would often include additional notes when she made the computer entry, it was for the best.

The grooming software had some other valuable features, including the ability to make and track appointments, set prices, collect payment information, and send automated email appointment reminders.

While it also provided some basic analytical features, the software was not an accounting system. Since we wanted to maintain good records for our business analysis and tax purposes, we also purchased easy-to-use accounting software. We imported the client records into the accounting software and were able to keep track of overall revenue as well as revenue by client. We also added vendors and vendor invoices to the accounting system so we could pay bills and track and analyze expenses. We ran monthly reports of revenue, expenses, and profits. Over time, we were able to run reports that compared revenue, expenses and profits from year to year. This was very helpful in analyzing our growth and determining what we needed to do to continue to grow the business.

Neither the grooming software nor the accounting software was very expensive – each cost a few hundred dollars – but the value of these systems? Priceless. We certainly could not have run a successful business without both software systems.

The lesson here: Regardless of the service business you want to operate, chances are you will be able to find specialized software for that business, or if not, a more generalized system that has most of the capabilities you need. We highly recommend acquiring a software system that facilitates running your particular business, even if you need to purchase separate accounting software, as we did. Having specialized software that automates the administrative and clerical aspects of your business will save you time and money in the long run, making it that much easier for you to concentrate on managing and growing the business instead of being bogged down with administration.

With our home office, the acquisition of the van, and our software systems, we were just about ready for business. But there were still a few operational details to work out before we could start marketing Bandanas.

Consider This...

Don't under-estimate the importance of your business structure, both from an ownership and liability perspective. Co-owning a business is a big responsibility, especially for a couple that has a personal as well as business relationship. Be honest with yourselves about who is best suited to be the primary owner. While every business decision should involve the two of you, there is likely to come a time when one person must make a final decision. Deal with this reality before it becomes a major issue for either one of you.

Any service you provide has a certain amount of risk. You may never think it could happen, but a client could refuse to pay a bill, go bankrupt, or threaten to sue your business. These types of issues are generally more easily dealt with if your business is an LLC or other form of corporation rather than a proprietorship.

When it comes to office space and outfitting your business, be reasonable and realistic. Some people who start businesses think they need to impress clients, so they rent expensive office space and outfit it with all the newest, latest equipment. They also may have the business lease a nice new car. These extravagances may make you feel good, but that feeling won't last for long if your expenses put you out of business. You can always upgrade to fancier office space and a nicer car when your business is established and you have clients who are paying you enough to cover such costs.

Instead of spending a lot of money early on, assume you will have minimal income from your service business in the first year. That's because you may very well need to spend that year building up your business. Work up a budget that includes rent and business assets that you can truly afford for one year, using startup capital from your own funds or a business loan. Your objective is to build the business in the first year so you can sustain it in year two and beyond.

We took a certain calculated risk when we started our business. We decided to purchase a $75,000 brand new specialized van to conduct mobile dog grooming and we had additional startup costs to operate the business. We self-funded the purchase of the van and all the other startup costs. We knew it would take some time to develop the business, so we set realistic expectations upfront. We anticipated that we would need several years of income from dog grooming before we would be able to pay ourselves back for the van. The fact that we were prepared for that reality took away some of the pressure of starting a business. We had confidence we would be successful, but we had enough money to cover our startup costs even if it took a whole year to acquire clients and generate a reasonable income stream. That reassurance allowed us to do the right things in the first year to grow the business.

Statistics on new business ownership are sobering, to say the least. Most startups generally follow the "80/20" rule, that is, 80 percent of new businesses typically fail within the first two to three years, while only 20 percent survive. If the business is run by you and your life partner, that is doubly disastrous, since a business failure affects income for both of you. To keep the odds in your favor and avoid being in the 80 percent, you need to have adequate funding for your business. Use conservative income projections and over-estimate startup expenses. The only surprise you want to get in the first year is a good one.

CHAPTER 4

Business Operations

Y ou know the old saying: "The devil is in the details." We had most of what we needed to launch our service business, but a few important details remained.

- It's natural to be excited about your new business – most business owners can't wait to start marketing their services. Still, it's important to have everything in place and all systems operating before you look for clients.

- Divvy up the responsibilities of running the business based on you and your partner's desires and skills. Work out these details in advance so there are no misunderstandings.

- Don't risk testing new systems on your clients. Be sure your phone number and message system work properly before launching your business. Script and record a professional sounding greeting for your message system. Be sure your website is fully functional and check for broken links. Send test emails prior to publicizing your email address.

- Pricing your service appropriately is essential. Pricing takes into consideration the type and level of service you provide as well as your competition. Pricing a service might also be based, in part, on what the market can bear.

As we started to think about what our business really involved, we thought it would be a good idea to break down the business into its logical "components" so we could establish a process for each component. This also helped us to discuss which of the components we would each be responsible for, and which we would collaborate on. Since we both are, to some extent, control freaks, clearly identifying the components of the business early on helped us set boundaries and maintain control of our respective areas.

These were the components we identified:

1. Our service – Dog grooming itself, the service we provided, and everything about it: what our services included, how our services were delivered and by whom, and what our services cost

2. Marketing – The brand – Bandanas Mobile Grooming – and the way we would launch the brand and promote it to prospective clients, including all marketing materials and media

3. Client support – The service we would provide during each groom, and also the way we would service the client before and after the groom

4. Business support – Everything required behind the scenes to support the business: the telephone system, the website and email system, the grooming software, the accounting software, banking, insurance, and regulatory and tax requirements

5. Supplies and maintenance – We recognized that our business would require constant replenishing of grooming supplies, sharpening of blades, and maintenance of the grooming equipment in the van as well as ongoing maintenance for the van itself.

With these components in mind, we divided up the responsibilities. Obviously, Sharon would be directly responsible for delivering our service. She was the person with dog grooming experience and the person who would perform the service and have contact with every client. We decided from the very start that she would be the face of Bandanas, and anything Barry would do would be accomplished in the background. In a service business, taking a very personal, one-to-one approach with clients is essential.

We both wanted to be actively involved in marketing the brand; however, we thought it would be best to adopt the "client/agency" role we felt comfortable with during our earlier experience of working together at Epsilon. In this case, Bandanas would be the client, represented by Sharon, and Barry would act as a 1-person agency. We would develop our brand marketing strategy together, but then Barry would execute the creative work and marketing program with Sharon's review and approval.

When it came to client support, we felt that Sharon should have primary responsibility. Barry would help with specific administrative tasks behind the scenes, though; for example, he would be responsible for sending appointment reminders via email to clients about a week before their appointments, and he would check the Bandanas email box and phone messages during the day, thus alleviating Sharon from administrative responsibility. We felt that this was a key to our success, since we wanted Sharon to spend as much time as possible grooming and generating revenue.

Barry would have primary responsibility for business support, so he would maintain the accounting system, handle the business details, and run reports, even though Sharon would enter information into the grooming software. Again, our objective was to make sure Sharon was devoting her time to grooming and servicing her clients rather than getting bogged down with business and administrative details. However, it was important that she make notations about each dog's attributes and the exact way she did each groom so she could use this information for subsequent grooms.

We did have to work out a little system later for recording client payments because of one interesting quirk. Sometimes, a client who paid for a groom by check wasn't home, so Sharon had to leave a payment envelope for the client to send the check later. Barry had to keep track of these client payments separately and let Sharon know when a client sent a check; if it wasn't received in a timely manner (which didn't happen very often), we would have to email or call the client.

Finally, supplies and maintenance became an area of joint responsibility. Sharon knew what supplies she needed, so she ordered them, or gave Barry a list of what she needed and he ordered them for her. A careful record was kept of all such expenses using our accounting software. Sharon and Barry shared the role of van maintenance, which turned out to be a significant, ongoing responsibility. Sharon was responsible for daily van maintenance, which involved cleaning the inside of the van, emptying the dirty water tank, and refilling the clean water tank. That got tiring, especially after a busy grooming day, so on occasion, Barry would help with the daily maintenance as well. Together, we "deep cleaned" the inside of the van and the dirty water tank on a quarterly basis and made appointments as needed to get the van serviced. It became obvious early on that the van required a lot of attention; after all, it was being utilized day in and day out for dog grooming, which is a dirty, hairy job! Without the van, we wouldn't have a business, so we took maintenance seriously. We also wanted to make sure it looked good, both outside and inside, to clients.

As you can see, we really tried to identify all the details of our working partnership so that we each knew what roles we had to play. Honestly, it wasn't always perfect – every once in a while, one of us would barge into each other's areas (accidentally or on purpose). That's what happens when you have two high-powered, high achieving people working together! But we always respected each other's "domains."

BANKING AND INSURANCE

When we first moved to Asheville, we established a relationship with a regional bank for our personal banking. We got to know the branch manager and liked the service the bank provided, so we felt comfortable continuing to use the same bank for our business. We established both a business checking account and a merchant credit card account. This gave us the ability to accept credit cards from clients and have the credit card fees taken directly out of our business checking account. We also got business credit cards from the bank to consolidate our business expenses and keep them separate from personal expenses.

Accepting credit cards was a very smart move for us. Even though we had to pay a percentage of each credit card sale to the bank, offering our clients this convenience became a value-added service that almost half of our clients used. It was a simple process for us to follow. Once Sharon got the credit card number and expiration date from the client, I called in that information, along with street address, zip code, and the amount charged to the card, to an automated phone service. In the rare instance when a charge was rejected, Sharon contacted the client and the problem was quickly resolved. In seven years of doing business, we never had a problem with a credit card payment or a check bouncing, for that matter. The only issue we'd have to resolve would be if a client had an updated expiration date or changed credit cards without informing us.

These days, small business owners have an even easier route to credit card services if they so desire: They can use "Square" or a similar service that makes accepting credit cards a snap. A Square mobile credit card reader plugs right into a smartphone. The business owner can then swipe any credit card, get a signature via the customer's finger, and have the payment authorized instantly, with a fee automatically deducted from any bank account. These kinds of systems offer convenience for both business owner and customer alike, and the fees can often be less than with a traditional bank.

Another relationship we established prior to forming Bandanas was with a local insurance agency. Since we were satisfied with the agency's service for our personal insurance, we asked if they could handle our business insurance as well. We obviously needed to insure the van and other physical assets, such as equipment, but doing so fell into the realm of commercial insurance, which is a lot more complicated than insuring a car or home for personal use. We also decided, after speaking with an attorney, that it would be wise to obtain professional liability insurance. The purpose of this insurance was to cover the business in the unlikely event that a dog should be injured or die during a groom. The insurance agency was helpful in obtaining a specialized commercial policy that combined both the van and liability insurance with one carrier.

Depending on the type of service business you operate and your financial needs, your relationship with a bank could be very important. In addition to business checking, merchant credit card services, and a business credit card, you might need a loan or a line of credit. Acquainting a bank's branch manager with your business will pay off in the long run. On the insurance side, you need to think about insuring any assets your business may have, as well as professional liability insurance, if appropriate. We had very specialized liability insurance because our business was dealing with live animals that could be injured. You need to determine if the service you provide has the kind of risk associated with it that would require insurance protection.

There were a few other business details that had to be taken care of before our business launch. We applied for a Federal ID number for the business which was necessary for tax and business identification purposes. We filed with the state of North Carolina's Department of Revenue so that we could pay state sales tax. Even though we were not required by North Carolina law to pay taxes on service revenue, we anticipated that, on rare occasion, we would purchase and resell a product to a client, such as a special shampoo, so we would need to collect sales tax on that sale. We also had to obtain a "privilege certificate" to do business with clients who lived in the city of Asheville.

GETTING READY TO GO ON THE ROAD

In the previous chapter, we discussed the grooming and accounting software we acquired. We wanted to be sure we fully understood the capabilities of the grooming software, so even before we got our first client, we entered a few simulated client and pet records and played around with the various features of the software. We decided not to use the system's automated email reminder system because it didn't seem personal enough; instead, we personalized each reminder and sent it manually via email. This was one of many personal touches that distinguished our service.

We discussed what kind of information we would need to monitor the business. We thought it would be a good idea to keep track of the number of clients, the number of pets, the pets per client, and the number of grooms per pet. We also wanted to know when someone became a client so we could track client longevity, and how often each pet was groomed so we could analyze frequency. All of this information was readily available via the grooming software.

From Sharon's perspective, it was just as important to keep excellent grooming records. Obviously, we needed to make sure we had the correct name, age, gender, and breed of each dog, as well as each client's name, address and contact information. But what really mattered to Sharon is that the software allowed her to keep very detailed information about grooming particulars: what the client (and the dog) did and did not like, the specific techniques, scissors, and clipper blades she used to do the groom, the type of shampoo and conditioner she used... even the type of bandana for each groom so she would use something different the next time! She would also record details about the names of her clients' other pets, spouses, and children. This was all so that she could remember a dog's particular personality, replicate a dog's groom each time, and maintain a close personal relationship with her clients by demonstrating an interest not just in their pets but in their lives.

On the financial side, we wanted to be able to see the income from the business as a whole on a monthly basis, as well as the income by client. We wanted to be aware of the level of income associated with each client, especially our major clients, so we could thank them periodically and give them special recognition during the holiday season. We also wanted to track our expenses, both by vendor and by category. One important task we needed to do was build a list of vendors for the various equipment and supplies we would need. We established accounts with key vendors, added them to our accounting system, and placed initial orders as needed. With the guidance of our accountant, we set up a chart of accounts using our accounting software and entered our initial expenses into the system.

We tested *everything!* We made sure our phone number worked, scripted and recorded a suitable greeting, called the number and left test messages, and then checked the messages to make sure they were received. We tested the contact form on our website to make sure it was funneling information to our email account, and we tested the email address from various computers to make sure the email was working properly.

The most important test, of course, was the van itself. Both of us drove around in the van to get accustomed to it. We devised a maintenance schedule so we would know what type of maintenance the van needed on a daily, weekly, monthly, quarterly, and annual basis. We tested all of the grooming equipment on our own dogs first and then cleaned up the van afterwards to see what that would involve. (Turns out one of our own dogs was a very challenging client!) Sharon did several grooms to make sure she was comfortable with all of the equipment. We found a storage facility not far from our home where we could park the van, as well as dispose of dirty water, fill our tank with clean water, and plug in an electrical cord so the van's inverter batteries could be charged overnight.

PRICING OUR SERVICE

One of the more challenging aspects of running a service business is determining how to price your service. When you sell products, you already know the cost. Basically, you resell the product with some standard markup you apply to cover your costs of doing business and allow for a reasonable profit. A service business is different. When you sell a service, you have to take into account all costs related to delivering that service, as well as your time (and if necessary, the time of others) involved in service delivery.

To price mobile dog grooming, we had to take into account the indirect cost of supplies, equipment, business costs, and operating the van. For the van, the biggest ongoing expense was diesel fuel. The Sprinter's diesel engine was very efficient, but diesel fuel costs more than gasoline, and we used a lot of it! In fact, the way the grooming systems were designed, we had to leave the van engine running during each groom to get either heat or air conditioning and to assist in keeping the inverter charged. In addition to the expenses associated with the grooming business, we obviously had to factor in Sharon's time as well as her expertise.

One thing we learned from running an agency was that the value of time varied greatly based on the expertise of the individual. In Barry's agency, for example, his time as the head of the agency was more valuable than an account executive's time. It was usually too complicated to charge a client for every individual's time, however, so more often than not, we used a "blended rate" for an agency hour that was comprised of certain percentages of the time of many people.

Thankfully, we didn't have that problem with Bandanas – Sharon was the only person selling her time, and my time was considered as a cost of doing business – but we did want to make sure she was fairly compensated for her expertise since she had ten years of experience and was a certified groomer. As a result, while the price for our service was based on a number of factors including the supplies we would have to use for a typical groom and the costs associated with doing a groom, the most important component of price was Sharon's time.

Unlike one of our primary competitors who charged by the hour, we decided to charge by the groom. We arrived at a minimum price for a full groom (bath, haircut, nails, bandana) that applied to the majority of dogs. We wanted our clients to feel confident that the price we quoted was the price we charged, period. For the most part, a groom could be completed in a little more than an hour or so, not including travel time. We did, however, charge a higher price for dogs that required considerable additional time. This included dogs that needed exacting haircuts, such as poodles, and dogs that were heavily matted.

Our price was higher than a retail grooming salon, but we felt it was justified, since we were providing an onsite service high in convenience and personalized service. Frankly, people who used mobile grooming could afford it. We periodically compared our price to other mobile groomers and found that we were competitive.

We also recognized that we would probably have to adjust our price in the future as our costs changed. In fact, during years when fuel costs were very high, we added a "fuel surcharge." For the most part, however, we were able to keep our price stable, with only a modest increase every few years. We wanted our clients to understand they were paying for a premium service, but we did not want them to think the price for grooming their dog was prohibitively expensive.

We recommend that you devote sufficient time to developing a sound pricing strategy. As we did, you should factor in the direct and indirect costs associated with delivering your service, as well as the expertise of the person(s) delivering the service. You should also consider the competitive environment and what the market can bear.

If you are delivering a professional service that is primarily time-based, you will probably sell your service one of two ways, either by the hour, or by the project. Each of these pricing strategies has unique advantages. Selling your time strictly by the hour can be advantageous when you are uncertain how long it will take to complete a client commitment and you want to be sure to be fairly compensated. Project pricing is attractive when you know a service you deliver might be more highly valued than the amount of time it takes you to complete the project; in other words, a project could result in a higher price-per-hour in certain circumstances.

As we discussed previously, direct and indirect costs should be factored into price, along with the value of an individual's time. A good rule of thumb in establishing an hourly rate is to charge between 1-1/2 to 2-1/2 times what your time would be worth if you were compensated as if you were an employee. For example, if your annual salary were to be $150,000, you would be paid $72 per hour, based on a 40-hour work week. That means your hourly rate in a service business would be somewhere between $108 and $180.

Working through what to charge is an extremely important component in a service business. Sometimes in a service business, you will find that there is a gap between perceived value and real value when it comes to setting prices. For example, consider a law firm that may have one or more "hotshot" principals. The more cases these attorneys win and the better they become known, the more likely it is that they will be able to set higher hourly fees than other attorneys, both inside and outside their firm, even if the actual number of years of experience they have is similar. That's because these individuals have a higher perceived value in the marketplace.

Make sure you consider both the perceived and real value of your service when you price it. If you have stellar credentials or extensive experience, you may be rightly justified to set a higher price than others who offer the same or a similar service. Still, you need to balance that against prices that are set by competitors in your line of business. At the same time, look at the aspects of your service business that make it unique, because those aspects may translate into setting a higher price. In our business, for example, bringing a completely equipped grooming salon to a client's door at a specified time and providing personal, one-to-one attention from an experienced professional who concentrates only on that client's dog is well worth a premium price to the target clientele.

Consider This...

For some entrepreneurs, there seems to be a certain amount of glory in taking a risk. While it is true that any couple who decides to start a business is taking some risk, we believe there is a difference between taking a calculated business risk and acting in a risky way. You can minimize your risk by understanding everything that is involved in running a service business upfront and by doing the right things to keep your risk low.

The "divide and conquer" strategy will help you minimize risk because you will have fewer disagreements and run your business with maximum efficiency. Determine what each of you does well and use that to guide the way you divide up responsibilities. A certain amount of overlap is healthy, but division of labor should be well thought out and lines of responsibility should be clearly defined. You don't want to be in a situation where one of you says, "I thought *you* were going to do that!" And you never want clients to pay a price for your uncertainty.

You can also lower your risk and optimize your chances for success by getting the right business partners to help you make smart decisions: an accountant, an attorney, an insurance agent, and a banker. Every entrepreneur, even those with lots of business experience, can benefit from wise counsel.

Another way to minimize risk is to spend time studying your market and your competition before you price your services. Develop a pricing strategy that considers many factors: your costs, your time, and your market. Your pricing should be fair but competitive. If you have considerable expertise in your service area, it is probably better to be a little on the high side rather than price your services too low or too high. Too low and you de-value your services – too high and you could price yourself out of your market. Remember to consider both perceived and real value in pricing your services. And if you offer a service that has unique aspects to it, you are probably in a position where you can set a premium price.

Should you ever negotiate on price? It depends. For a very large project, or to obtain a lot of ongoing work, you could consider a "courtesy discount." Part of the decision to discount rests on how important it is to win a particular piece of business. Discounting could set a precedent, however. Word could get around that you discounted your services, and then you might find out that a new client expects the same consideration. In general, keeping your prices consistent across clients is probably the best pricing strategy. Offering a fair but competitive price works out to your benefit and to a client's benefit. As we'll discuss later, one very important aspect of a service business is keeping clients happy so they will refer other clients to you – and setting a fair price is one sure way to keep them happy.

CHAPTER 5

Launching the Business

Y ou have the money you need to establish your business. You've set up your office and acquired the necessary business assets. You figured out who's going to do what and how to price your service. Now it's time to go out and get clients.

- Your business is also your brand. A strong brand is comprised of a good name, a logo, appropriate brand positioning, and a solid brand promise.

- Marketing your brand effectively is crucial to your service business. Once you determine your target audience, you'll need to use the most appropriate methods to generate awareness and encourage usage of your service.

- It helps to build a profile of your ideal client and picture him or her in your mind. This makes it easier to develop the right branding approach and appropriate messaging to reach that person.

- Providing a service rather than selling a product implies that you are seeking to acquire a "client" – someone whose business you cultivate over time – instead of a "customer." Meeting that client's needs time and time again, and getting that client to become a "fan" who refers others, is something that will greatly contribute to your business success.

Once we had decided on a name for our dog grooming business, we knew we needed a brand identity – even before we had purchased the van.

Our experience working in a direct marketing agency environment, and Barry's subsequent experience in a brand-oriented ad agency, made us aware of just how important "branding" would be; in fact, from the very beginning, we wanted to establish a brand that made Bandanas Mobile Grooming Salon look very professional. Fact is, we wanted to be a "cut above" the competition.

We knew we had to build our brand around a strong logo. We looked at other mobile grooming operations both locally and elsewhere and noticed that the majority of them relied on cartoon-style illustrations to promote their businesses. Even the leading mobile dog grooming franchise in the country used this style of illustration. We wanted to look different, and it was very important to us that an upscale clientele found our brand appealing.

Sharon had a good idea of what she wanted for a logo: a dog wearing a Western-style red bandana. This made sense for two reasons: First, putting bandanas on dogs after grooming is pretty much a standard practice for most every groomer. But for us, it was a particularly important part of our service given our business name.

Second, our location was Western North Carolina. Although this area of the country isn't equivalent to "cowboy country," it is the western-most part of the state, and there is a certain rugged, outdoor quality to the land and the people who live here. Dogs seem to enjoy and participate in the area's recreational opportunities as much as their owners – they accompany their humans on walks, runs, hikes, and bikes and are often seen walking with their owners on city streets and in city parks. To us, a dog in a Western-style bandana represented this type of lifestyle.

Using Sharon's conceptual idea as a guide, we contracted with an online logo service and gave them some basic direction about the concept we had in mind. The logo service came back to us with three different designs, one of which we liked immediately. It was a simple yet elegantly drawn illustration of the head of a smiling black-and-white dog with a prominent red bandana around its neck. The bottom of the bandana touched and subtly overlapped one of the letters in the word BANDANAS, with the words Mobile Grooming Salon in smaller type below it. It was also a plus that the logo used just two colors, black and red. The logo was exactly the feel we wanted: Friendly and approachable yet classy and upscale, and we immediately recognized the value of having red as a strong primary color to distinguish our business.

The Bandanas Logo
(shown in black-and-white; bandana would be red)

We then talked about the possibility of using a slogan. We thought a catchy slogan might set us apart from other businesses, especially if it helped define the advantage of using our service. In writing our business plan, we used this positioning to describe the business: "Bandanas Mobile Grooming Salon is a self-contained pet grooming salon on wheels providing the quality of a professional retail grooming establishment with come-to-the-customer convenience." Based on this positioning, we brainstormed about slogans and finally decided on this one:

Lookin' Good in Your Neighborhood

This slogan reinforced the friendly personality we wanted clients to associate with the business, and it highlighted our primary attribute: Bandanas comes to you to make your dog look good.

The very first thing we did with the logo and the slogan was provide these elements to the company that was detailing the van. We anticipated that the van itself would be our biggest and most prominent piece of advertising – kind of like a billboard on wheels – so we decided on a white van and told the company we wanted the black-and-red logo to appear on every surface of the van – front back, and both sides. From our direct marketing background, we knew it would be essential for someone who saw the van driving by to see our contact information, so we had both our phone number and website address prominently displayed on all van surfaces as well, using red for the phone number and black for the website address. Our slogan could be seen across the top left and right side and on the back door of the van in red.

Let's put what we did into a broader context. There are three main elements in creating the service brand: the brand name, the brand logo, and the brand slogan. Each of these elements stands alone but works in concert to make for a strong brand.

1. Brand Name

Naming the brand obviously comes first and it is no easy task. In many respects, it is easier to name a product than it is to name a service business. Some classes of service businesses, particularly professional service firms, choose brand names that incorporate their own surnames. This is a common practice among law firms, accounting firms, marketing firms, and consultants. While there is nothing wrong with this practice and it may be appropriate for some service businesses, it does nothing to distinguish the business from a marketing perspective. The fact is, in a service business, the name of the business is the primary brand. Why not take advantage of the marketing potential of a brand name that represents something meaningful about the business?

Some of the things you need to consider in naming your business are:

• The nature of your business and the service sector you are in, such as financial services, pet services, travel services, etc.

• The unique qualities of your service and how they might translate into a suitable name

• Differentiation: You want to differentiate yourself from your competitors as well as be sure the name you select is available and does not conflict with any other similar name. You can easily do an online national trademark search through the U.S. Patent and Trademark Office (www.uspto.gov) to determine if a name is available for use. While it is not always essential to trademark the name of a service business, it may be wise to do so to protect your brand name. An excellent booklet that explains Federal trademark protection, *Protecting Your Trademark*, is available from the USPTO. Also, it is a good idea to check any brand name to determine if it is available as a domain name. Enter "domain name search" in any search engine and you will find numerous free sources available for instantly checking domain names. Purchasing a domain name is one of the first things you should do when you create a brand name.

The best brand names, whether they are businesses or products, are memorable and meaningful. Your brand name needs to attract and hold the attention of your target audience. Ideally, it should reflect what your business stands for, or possibly a compelling benefit.

Creating a brand name is part art and part science. Brainstorming names is a good way to start. There are numerous online resources available for creating names, including naming agencies and online services that "crowdsource" names (services that charge fairly reasonable fees for others to come up with possible names).

2. Brand Logo

Think of the brand logo as a graphic representation of the brand name. It often includes a graphic image or symbol and employs colors that will consistently be used in portraying the brand. Sometimes, the manner in which type is used, or the use of a unique typeface can be a logo (often referred to as logotype). Does a service business need a logo? Yes and no. In our case, a logo – our dog wearing the bandana – was an essential part of our service. It graphically represented the service we offered and it was eye-catching as well. Looking at our logo on the side of our van from a distance, you could make a good guess as to the type of business we were in, even if you couldn't read the business name.

The Bandanas logo was also the type of logo that could easily be produced, since it was a line illustration (no use of screens) executed in just two colors. With advances in color technology, you could easily use more than two colors, but every color adds complexity to a logo. You will notice that the best logos tend to be simply executed. The mark of a good logo is that it looks great even in one color, and it can be reproduced at virtually any size without a loss of quality.

Give some thought as to whether a logo is necessary to enhance the brand of your service business. The decision to use a logo has implications: it is best created by a professional logo designer and, once created, its usage must be carefully managed.

3. Brand Slogan

A brand slogan is a short statement, often a phrase, that characterizes the brand in a certain way. As with the brand logo, the brand slogan is not mandatory, but a brand slogan accomplishes something important: it sets the tone for your business. In fact, a brand slogan can really establish the *position* of a brand – that means how the brand is perceived in the mind of a prospect, and how the brand fits when a prospect compares it to competing brands. A strong business slogan can be timeless, such as "Just Do It" for Nike or "I'm Lovin' It" for McDonald's. These phrases have been used by these companies for many years as "tag lines" in major advertising campaigns. They are worded so that they embody the personalities of the companies.

Sometimes, marketers talk about brand slogans that are "aspirational." This means the slogan, and the brand itself for that matter, should make the brand user want to aspire to something. In Nike's case, "Just Do It" can mean a lot of things, but it directly relates to the overall aspiration of Nike's core audience – committed athletes of any kind – who are competitive and will do whatever it takes to compete successfully.

The Bandanas slogan, "Lookin' Good in Your Neighborhood," was not as much an aspirational statement as it was a statement of a specific service benefit. For our service business, we felt creating a benefit-oriented slogan was the most effective approach. Whichever approach you take, if you decide to use a slogan, make sure that your slogan is appropriate for your target audience.

MARKETING THE BRAND

Next on the branding agenda for us was building our brand identity. While Barry's primary skill was on the copy side, he had a good eye for design, so he created a business card, letterhead and envelope, incorporating the logo and slogan into each printed element. We discussed the other types of marketing materials we might need. Given that we planned to focus on an upscale clientele, we thought it would be important to produce a high quality brochure. We used photos that the detailing company provided of the van, and took a photo of Sharon in a red shirt and black pants with our own dogs.

Barry wrote the copy and laid out the brochure. It was an 8-page, full color, pamphlet size piece printed on coated stock that could be handed out or mailed in a 6 by 9-inch envelope. The copy talked about the benefits of using Bandanas, detailed everything that was included in a groom, and highlighted Sharon's grooming experience. We also included a few "before" and "after" photos of dogs Sharon had groomed to show the dramatic difference a grooming could make.

The red shirt and black pants that Sharon wore in the brochure photo ultimately became part of the Bandanas brand in a modified way. Early on, we got the idea to have our logo embroidered onto a gray shirt. We purchased a few of the shirts, but then we realized Sharon needed many shirts to get through a week of dog groom-ing! We decided not to spend the extra money on embroidered logos; instead, we found a red shirt with white and black trim. This shirt, with black pants, became Sharon's standard uniform, adding to the consistency of our brand image. It reminded us of UPS or FedEx – two outstanding companies who use vans in their businesses and always wear uniforms as part of their brands.

Our other primary promotional tool was a website. In keeping with the look and feel of the van and the brochure, the website was executed on a white background with black type, using red as a secondary color. The van was prominently featured on the home page. We decided to put an educational spin on the site. We wanted clients to fully understand the benefits of mobile dog grooming, so we included a "grooming guide" with helpful information for consumers, whether or not they decided to use our service. We thought this would help position us differently from the competition since most of the competitive websites were nothing more than a one- or two-page sales pitch; in fact, we noticed that many mobile groomers didn't even have websites.

A key element of our website that really helped distinguish us was a "virtual tour" of our grooming van. Barry took photos of Sharon grooming one of our own dogs – he happened to be a white West Highland terrier, so he fit beautifully into our color scheme! (Behind the scenes, however, this little guy was not the most cooperative model to work with, and grooming him was a testament to Sharon's patience and calm demeanor.) We then organized the photos so they would represent all of the phases of our grooming process, from the time a dog steps into the van until the dog gets his complimentary bandana. In this way, website visitors could experience a simulated groom and feel comfortable with the way we operated.

We were very careful in how we applied the logo and slogan to all our brand elements. We maintained consistency in the use of the logo, the color red, and the typeface. We also tried to establish a copy style and tone that represented Bandanas. The copy was friendly and informal, yet professional and respectful of the reader. We always focused on the benefits of mobile dog grooming and what made us different, while reinforcing the high quality service we provided.

As for launching our business, we followed a very simple plan. First, we wrote a feature article about the business and sent it along with a picture of the van to the editor of a small weekly newspaper that was delivered in our target communities. This was the type of newspaper that was always looking for local community news, so a well-written article had a good chance of getting printed. In fact, the article ran verbatim on the front page, along with a photo of the van!

Then we put our brochure into an envelope, accompanying it with a printed letter that offered a 10 percent discount to new customers. We drove around several of our target communities and inserted the envelope into newspaper boxes (not mailboxes, which would have required an addressed, stamped envelope). We weren't shy about driving around the communities in the van since that was the best piece of advertising we had. You just couldn't miss our logo, website address, and phone number. These few activities generated enough inquiries via phone and through our website contact form to result in our first few clients. In the next chapter, we'll talk more about how these clients became our real launching pad for business success.

UNDERSTANDING OUR AUDIENCE

How did we arrive at the branding approach we followed? Basically, it revolved around a timeless direct marketing principle: Understanding our audience. When we first conceived of the business, we discussed who our typical customer might be. Obviously the person was a dog owner, but it had to be someone who would find a mobile dog grooming service of great value. We made the following assumptions:

1. The person didn't have time to drop off and pick up the dog at a retail grooming location, and probably didn't want to leave the dog there for a lengthy period of time. For this person, a mobile dog grooming service had high perceived value.

2. The person was willing to pay more to have a dog grooming service come to their home. Being able to afford mobile dog grooming suggested that the individual would have a moderate to high income and likely live in an upscale community. A higher demographic suggested home ownership, a higher level of education, and success in a business or profession.

3. The dog owner was likely to be a middle-aged woman who, as part of her household responsibilities, got the dog groomed. This turned out to be perhaps a little more targeted than necessary, since the age range was broader. However, most of the customers were women.

4. The dog was integrated into family life and was a member of the household. This would be especially true if the dog required grooming regularly rather than just a few times a year. It was essential for us to recognize that the dog was often regarded not just as a pet, but truly a member of the family. It wouldn't be crazy to state that Sharon had to imagine herself as a personal hair stylist for a family member!

By developing this profile of a typical client, we were able to picture someone in our mind and target that individual with the branding elements we developed – the brand name, logo, slogan, brand identity, and collateral materials. Just as important, that profile helped us establish our service area; in fact, we were able to target very specific residential communities where there were likely to be a large concentration of prospective clients.

When we first explored moving to Asheville, we found that local zoning laws seemed to be less strict than in Massachusetts. We noticed, for example, that industrial buildings could border residential areas, and that residential housing could be intermingled with commercial businesses. As a result, distinct communities (sometimes known as "developments") were created as a way to establish residential neighborhoods, restrict commercial business, and maintain property values. These communities were often identified by name, so they were easy to find. Each community had its own unique attributes, and some communities were gated. (As an aside, a peculiarity of the Asheville area is that many communities and businesses use "Biltmore" in their names, since Asheville is the home of Biltmore, the country's largest private home and a major tourist attraction. This fact can create significant confusion for people who are not familiar with the area; for example, two residential communities, "Biltmore Park" and "Biltmore Lake" are in different locations, neither of which is very close to Biltmore itself.)

We moved to a community located to the south of Asheville. Asheville is a relatively small metropolitan area, so we could get into downtown Asheville in about fifteen minutes. As we got to know the area, we realized that there were several such communities located in close proximity to one another. We decided to concentrate our business on these south Asheville communities in the hope that we would develop a large enough clientele without having to expand our geographic radius. This had two benefits: First, the business would be located close to where we lived, which cut down on Sharon's commuting time, and second, it would be much more efficient if Sharon's service area was tightly defined. In mobile dog grooming, you can spend considerable time driving from one client to another. This translates into fewer grooms per day and higher fuel costs. If we were able to make the geographic constraint pay off, we thought we would improve our chances for success. And, if this strategy didn't produce enough clients, we could always expand our service area.

Thankfully, the strategy worked very well. Sharon was able to grow and service a clientele that resided in or near about five residential communities, and these communities were all within less than a ten-mile radius. Concentrating our business in this tightly defined geographic area also helped us target our marketing efforts.

"CUSTOMER" VS. "CLIENT"

Our experience in direct marketing taught us another important lesson: Many businesses acquire at a loss and renew at a profit. This simple principle applies broadly, regardless of business type. What it means is that the money you spend to acquire a new customer usually exceeds the business you get from the first sale. Rather it is the second and subsequent sales that make money. It is always challenging to get a new customer, so a business often must invest more to acquire a new customer than that customer is actually worth on the first sale. Since the business has to spend much less on subsequent sales from the same customer, a customer becomes profitable from the second sale onward. The real implication here is that *retaining a customer* becomes essential if a business is to succeed.

That's why we considered someone who used our service the first time a "customer." Our job was to convert that customer into a "client" – a person who relied on Bandanas time after time, providing us with the revenue that represented "renewal at a profit." As we learned in the agency business, a "client" is much more valuable than a "customer." When you think of a customer as a client, you think about what you need to do to cultivate a long-term relationship. You also recognize that being in a service business means *providing* service in the true sense of the word, as in servicing a client's needs. What's more, satisfied clients very often refer additional business to you.

In the next chapter, we'll talk more specifically about the kinds of things we did to turn customers into clients – how we used certain tactics to meet the needs of our clients, make them feel special, and encourage them to make referrals. But for now, we can tell you without a doubt that it was the quality of our service and the way Sharon treated her clients that helped us build, grow and sustain a successful service business.

Consider This...

In a service business, *you* are part of the brand. Bandanas was very fortunate in that Sharon was not only an experienced, qualified dog groomer, she also had been a marketing and sales professional in her previous career. This gave her the ability to understand her clients' needs, converse with them and make them feel comfortable, and follow up with them after a groom. Those qualities gave us a real service advantage. Think about your own personal brand – your appearance, your mannerisms, your ability to interact with a client, and your follow-through skills. These things could play a large role in determining whether your service business achieves the success you want.

Make a strong brand a priority. Sometimes, a service business owner makes the mistake of thinking branding a service business is not essential – that's only necessary for products. In our view, branding a service business helps solidify it in a prospective client's mind and differentiates it from the competition. Our brand, Bandanas Mobile Grooming Salon, was distinctive, and we were able to build a strong brand identity around it. We believe the brand was part of the reason our service business succeeded.

Barry had worked in a strategic and creative capacity at several agencies, so he knew what it took to develop and build a brand identity. He approached branding Bandanas much as he would a "real" client. Not everyone has this expertise – so don't try to execute your brand yourself unless you have this skill set. You would do well to engage a small agency or a designer who has experience doing branding and corporate identity. Investing in one or more professionals who can create your brand and execute it in a variety of formats will pay off in the long run.

Remember the difference between a customer and a client. If you treat every customer like a client, and do the kinds of things it takes to gain a client's confidence, you will have a much better chance of keeping that client over the long haul, as well as having that client refer others to you.

In a service business, a happy client is the bottom line. Acquiring clients who are the right fit and retaining the right clients is really what your business is all about.

CHAPTER 6

The Business of Service

Marketing a service business is based on building relationships. Unlike selling a product, in selling a service, you have to be able to represent and deliver an intangible. This is why the focus of a service business is truly on the concept of "service."

- Set the tone for a successful relationship from the very beginning by showing clients their continuing business is important to you.
- Find ways to make clients feel important and special. Always be authentic in showing that you care about your clients. Even little things can make a big difference.
- Communicate with clients periodically. Provide them with information of value that relates to your service and it will keep your business top of mind.
- Monetary profit is important, but so is "psychic profit." Consider using a service business for a different kind of service – to serve your community. Community service has its own rewards that you can share together, and it may even pay you back in unexpected ways.

In the previous chapter, we discussed how we built our brand and launched Bandanas Mobile Grooming. We mentioned that we acquired our first clients using three basic methods: getting an article about Bandanas placed in a small community newspaper, distributing our brochure to target communities via paper boxes, and riding around those communities in our "moving billboard," the van.

These simple activities resulted in a handful of clients who in a sense became our "charter" clients – the very first clients who believed enough in mobile dog grooming to give it a try. We recognized that they were, to some extent, taking a leap of faith by using Bandanas and we had to build immediate trust. While the introductory discount we offered may have drawn attention to our service and promoted a trial, we had to make sure every one of our new clients stayed with us beyond one groom and became a raving fan. We remembered the reality of "renewal at a profit."

Sharon's approach with these clients set the tone for the relationship. Once we received a lead, Sharon called each prospective client and engaged them in a phone conversation about their dog. As a dog lover herself, Sharon knew that anyone who invested in regular dog grooming was likely to treat their pet as part of the family. She acknowledged this special relationship by establishing a rapport, asking about the dog and sharing her own experiences with dogs, in particular, the breed of dog the client owned. Barry eavesdropped on some of these conversations and was amazed at the way Sharon made someone she never met feel immediately comfortable.

Sharon quickly qualified the client as well. If the dog didn't seem like a suitable match for our service, she would refer the prospect to another mobile dog groomer or suggest retail grooming as an option. Early on, Sharon had decided that it would not be feasible to groom certain dogs. For the most part, she eliminated from consideration any dog over 60 pounds and dogs she knew from experience would be too challenging in a mobile dog grooming environment. Huskies, for example, did not like to be in an enclosed space, so they would not be good candidates for mobile dog grooming.

If the dog was a good candidate for our service, Sharon continued chatting informally, but at the same time, she collected specific information, writing it down on a "client intake form" we had developed. This information would be the basis for a client record in our grooming system. In addition, she was able to use the information she collected to provide a price estimate on the phone, further qualifying the client. We did not want the client to be surprised by the cost of mobile dog grooming. She always qualified the price by saying she would have to see the dog and evaluate its condition before establishing a firm price.

If the client was amenable to the price estimate, Sharon would set up an appointment. If appropriate, this appointment would be a no-obligation "meet and greet," during which time Sharon would meet the client and her dog, discuss the grooming process, and show the client the van, but not actually do a groom. The majority of the time, however, the client felt comfortable enough after the phone conversation to proceed with making an appointment for the dog's first groom.

FIRST IMPRESSIONS ARE LASTING

Everything in a service business is about first impressions. We hoped that our brochure and website made a good first impression – good enough for a prospective client to contact us in the first place. We hoped Sharon's friendly, professional announcement on our phone line – the first Bandanas voice the prospect heard – encouraged the prospective client to leave a message. Then, we wanted the prospective client to get a good first impression of the service we could provide by having an engaging phone conversation with Sharon.

All of these "firsts" built up to the most important first – the first impression of the groomer and the van. For that first grooming appointment, Sharon established a way of doing business that we hoped would impress the client. She made sure she knew exactly where the client's home was located and arrived a few minutes earlier than her scheduled appointment time. She drove up in her handsome clean white van, wearing her red and black Bandanas uniform. She made sure she allotted some additional time for the first groom so she could chat with the client beforehand.

One of the key elements of the first groom was the way in which Sharon greeted and interacted with the client's dog. Sharon has a natural positive, calm energy that seems to immediately put dogs at ease. She recognizes that dogs can be apprehensive about going into a strange vehicle with an unfamiliar person.

During the first visit, Sharon spoke with the owner about what the grooming process involved while the dog was at her side, assessing the dog's affect and behavior. She then diplomatically suggested that the owner return to her house, since she found that dogs tended to be more anxious and could act up if the owner was present. Sharon then calmly led the dog into the van, or carried it if it was too small to go up the step. She let the dog sniff around for a while to get acquainted.

We won't go into the specifics of the grooming process, which would be of limited interest to anyone except a dog groomer; however, we do want to make a few important points from a service perspective. We regarded the dog, not just the person, as a client. When the dog was in the van, Sharon did everything possible to ensure that her canine client had a positive grooming experience. She would make sure the temperature was comfortable, play music, and sometimes even spray a natural anti-anxiety fragrance into the air. She worked slowly, calmly, and methodically. If everything went well, the dog would grow accustomed to Sharon and the van, and that meant subsequent grooms would be that much faster, easier and without stress. Also, the dog would return from a groom giving off positive energy, which would make the owner feel good.

Making sure the groom went well was easier said than done. The fact is, while the groomer goes through the same basic steps to groom each dog, every dog is different. For example, some dogs are very nervous while others are calm. Some don't like having their nails trimmed while others don't like the sound of the dryer. Some dogs don't want you anywhere near their tails. This is why Sharon's calm, positive energy was so important. Some dogs simply require a lot more patience than others!

At the end of the groom, Sharon lightly sprayed the dog with a fresh scent and tied a bandana around its neck. This is a standard practice with most groomers. But she added a few extras that differentiated our service.

She filled out a special printed form we had created that provided the dog's owner with a "report card" about the groom. Using check boxes, Sharon would indicate which services she performed and then she would write down any notes about the dog's behavior during the groom or any skin issues she had noticed. The form included a spot where she could suggest a timeframe for the dog's next groom, or write in the dog's next appointment, if the date had already been set. The form also had an area that we used to record a check or credit card payment, so the form acted as a receipt for the service as well.

When she returned the dog to the owner, Sharon handed the owner the report form, along with a gourmet dog treat, packaged in a plastic envelope. The envelope was sealed with a sticker that read, "Compliments of Bandanas Mobile Grooming Salon," along with our logo. The form and the dog treat never failed to impress a client.

Some clients would have Sharon groom their dogs when they were not home. Sharon would either have a key or a code to enter the home, get the dog and groom it, and return the dog and lock up. In these cases, she would leave the groom report and the dog treat for the client and, if the client needed to pay by check, she would also leave behind a stamped, self-addressed envelope for the client's convenience.

These two enhancements to our service – the groom report and the gourmet dog treat – did not add much time or cost to each groom. What they provided, though, was evidence that our client service was indeed a cut above. As insignificant as they may seem, the groom report and gourmet dog treat differentiated our service from other mobile dog groomers, sending the subtle message that maybe we cared about our clients a little bit more.

SERVICING THE CLIENT

When Sharon returned the dog to the owner, handing her the groom report and the dog treat, she also attempted to secure the next appointment if one hadn't already been made. For a new client, the second appointment was crucial, because remember, a first time "customer" doesn't really become a "client" until there is an ongoing relationship.

Whether or not the new client made an appointment at that time, Sharon thanked her for the business. The next day, Barry generated a personalized letter to the new client, welcoming her and her dog as a Bandanas client and thanking her for the business. Also in that letter was an offer: We told the client that if she were to refer a new client to Bandanas, the new client would get a 10 percent discount on the first groom. If the new client mentioned the name of the referring client, that person would get 10 percent on her next groom as well. We always made good on this promise. One note here: Even though all of our clientele were upscale consumers who didn't really need the 10 percent discount, this approach still worked. Sometimes, a price discount is irresistible, no matter what income bracket you're in!

We found that, over the years, our two largest sources of business were direct and indirect referrals. Direct referrals resulted from one client referring another client to us. Obviously, this was the best kind of business to acquire, since it meant we had a client who was satisfied enough to refer someone else to Bandanas. The referring client became our sales agent, and the referral was an endorsement, which made our selling job much easier. Referrals from clients tend to be individuals who are neighbors or who are at least at the same economic level as the referring client, so they are large pre-qualified as good prospects.

Indirect referrals came from someone in a neighborhood seeing the Bandanas van and calling us up. More often than not, when Sharon asked where our van had been seen, she was able to say to the prospective client, "Oh yes, I groom Sally Jones' dog Fluffy on your block" or something similar, so there was an immediate connection. Occasionally, a prospect outside of a community would call because of seeing the van on the road, but if that person did not live in one of our target communities, we would politely decline the business and refer the person elsewhere.

The client welcome letter was just the beginning of a relationship we cultivated. We asked every client for their email address and virtually everyone complied, so we could use email as our primary means of communicating. We set up a little system so that Barry would check Sharon's appointment calendar the week prior to client grooms. He would then send personalized emails to the appropriate clients reminding them of their upcoming appointments. Several clients commented about how useful they found these reminders. It also helped our business, since it drastically reduced the number of people forgetting their appointments and not being home. We had heard from some groomers in both retail and mobile environments that "no-shows" could be a chronic problem, but with our reminder system, that wasn't an issue for us.

We also created a quarterly email newsletter called "Clippings" to send to clients. In it, we discussed shedding, skin conditions, and other grooming-related information. Sometimes, we listed places to take dog hikes or mentioned an adoption sale at our local humane society. While we just intended for the newsletter to be value-added information as part of our service, it often triggered several clients contacting us to make their next appointments. This reminded us of the old adage that a client isn't always thinking about you – you have to make an on-going effort to stay in front of the client.

Each year during the holiday season, we did something special for our clients. Every client's dog got a holiday bandana and a holiday dog treat. For those clients who didn't have grooms scheduled during the holidays, we would deliver the bandanas and treats to their door. For the clients who had been most active and had been with us the longest, we would do something even more special. One year, we delivered a package of assorted dog bakery treats to each major client; another year, we gave each of them a packet of blank greeting cards with amusing dog illustrations on the covers, created by a local artist.

If a client's dog passed away, which was inevitable with older dogs, Sharon would not only send a condolence card, she would make a donation in the dog's name to the local humane society.

To reinforce business continuity and add to our differentiation in the first few years, we created a kind of frequent buying club which we called "Bandanas Best Buddies." Every client who had their dog groomed six or more times annually received a membership card (with the dog's name on it, of course). This meant Fido was honored as a Bandanas Best Buddy! We arranged with a local dog bakery to offer a discount to any member who showed the card, and we offered a 10 percent discount on every sixth groom. While we loved the idea, quite honestly it became a logistical problem once we acquired many clients, so we phased it out over time.

We also gave serious consideration to selling products. At one point early on, we thought of creating a "Bone of the Month Club." Our idea was to deliver bones, dog treats, food or other merchandise to clients on a monthly basis – but as the grooming business itself grew, we quickly abandoned this concept. We thought it just would have been too time-consuming to make special deliveries. Instead, we offered a limited number of grooming-related products to our clients, such as specialty shampoos, conditioners and fragrances that clients could use between grooms. Sales of these products never contributed very much to our bottom line, but they were just another example of offering a little something extra for the convenience of our clients. We thought about private labeling these products with our own logo, but that never came to pass.

All of the little things we did – filling out a groom report, offering a gourmet dog treat, sending a reminder email, offering discounts for referrals, presenting clients with a holiday gift, whatever it might be – were designed with one thing in mind: Providing the best service possible to each client. We felt that little things would make a big difference.

Perhaps the most interesting lesson we learned about service, however, is that being authentic and caring about clients trumps everything else. Sharon really got to know her clients and she cared about their dogs. She went out of her way to make the dogs feel comfortable during a groom, even if it meant giving a dog a special treat; for one especially difficult dog client, for example, Sharon brought along pieces of hot dog so she could reward him for cooperating. This dog was a biter until Sharon started feeding him hot dogs!

Our clients often treated Sharon as part of the family. Some clients would not just talk to her about their dogs, they would share stories about their families and children. Some clients would ask her about their dogs' health or habits (Sharon was always careful to deflect serious health issues to a veterinarian), or for pet sitter and kennel recommendations. When you gain this kind of trust and respect from a client, you know you have succeeded in building a very special service business.

You may legitimately wonder if all the attention we gave to existing clients paid off. Without question, we think it did. As we said earlier, we knew from our experience in direct marketing that the cost associated with retaining an existing client is far less than the cost of acquiring a new client. We witnessed this first-hand, time and time again across various industries, so to us, investing in keeping clients happy – and maintaining their business for as long as possible – made a lot of sense. The ongoing business of these clients was directly responsible for the success of Bandanas, not just because they kept coming back year after year, but also because of their value as an indirect sales force for our business. We had a very high client retention rate over the years, and we saw the direct impact our existing clients had on new client acquisition via referrals. The satisfied clients who continued to do business with us helped make it almost unnecessary for us to invest marketing dollars in new client acquisition. Most of our business came from word of mouth.

SERVICE TO THE COMMUNITY

We want to talk a little bit about another aspect of a service business that should not be overlooked: service to the community. We believe running a service business presents a unique opportunity to not only make a monetary profit, but to make a "psychic profit" by helping the community in which you live and giving back to others. That was part of what we wanted to achieve as owners of a service business.

Given our mutual passion for dogs and animals in general, we wanted Bandanas to be a giving member of the local animal welfare community. Obviously, this was a perfect fit, especially since Asheville is a very animal-oriented city. Our business was built around people who could afford to have their dogs groomed at a premium price, so we felt it would be personally rewarding to find ways for Bandanas to give back to animals who were not so fortunate. We decided that we would contribute some of Bandanas' profits to support homeless and needy animals cared for by Asheville Humane Society, the nonprofit organization that ran the county's animal shelter. We also gave money to Chain-Free Asheville, an organization that helped convince people to get their dogs off of chains by building fences for them, free of charge. Eventually, Chain-Free Asheville was able to get a city ordinance passed that banned chaining within city limits.

There was more to it than money, however. Sharon and I both decided to volunteer with Asheville Humane Society. While we each played different roles, Sharon used her specialized skill to groom shelter dogs on a volunteer basis. In fact, she devoted one day a week to grooming at the shelter. Her greatest satisfaction was to take a dirty, terribly matted stray and magically transform this "mess" into a clean, groomed dog, ready to be adopted. Little did we know that her voluntary service would turn into a whole different kind of opportunity. More about that later!

Perhaps the most rewarding community service experience we had during our early Bandanas years, though, was as volunteer groomers at an animal shelter in a neighboring county. For years, this private shelter had been taking in too many animals. The space was inadequate and the conditions were deplorable. Authorities finally stepped in to seize the shelter and a massive cleanup took place, supported by local and national organizations and volunteers.

We volunteered the use of the Bandanas van so we could bathe the animals onsite in preparation for them to be sent to other shelters around the country. We didn't really know what we were getting ourselves into. We ended up bathing more than thirty neglected, dirty pit bulls over the course of two days. It was exhausting but worth it.

This was our first up-close interaction with pit bulls. They were a rarity in Massachusetts but were plentiful in North Carolina. We had been aware of their reputation as a "bully breed," and we were somewhat apprehensive about the task. It turned out, though, to be incredibly satisfying. We shared the work, bathing and drying the pit bulls. We stayed calm and did not exhibit any fear. These big beauties, neglected though they were, turned out to be as gentle and friendly as could be. They were directly responsible for changing our perception about pit bulls. Despite the fact that they had been poorly cared for, these pitties were some of the sweetest and trusting dogs we had ever met.

The experience helping these animals in need was an unexpectedly gratifying aspect of owning a service business together: feeling good about serving our own community.

Consider what role your service business could play in your community. Unlike us, you don't necessarily have to get involved in a cause that directly relates to your business. Pick something you're passionate about. It could be helping animals, helping kids, helping patients in a hospital, or helping residents in a retirement home. Whatever it is, set aside some time to perform community service and do something good for your local area. You likely will find that it isn't just rewarding for you, it is also a very sound business strategy.

Consider This...

You and your partner are not only running a service business, you are in the business of service. When you broaden your definition of service, it means much more than the service your business provides.

Service also means the manner in which you service your clients – all of the little things you do to encourage repeat business and maintain an ongoing relationship. It means valuing client relationships enough to take a personal interest in a client's needs and wants. It means developing an approach that preserves continuity with a client. It means providing the kind of service that is so exceptional a client becomes a fan and enthusiastically refers friends, acquaintances, colleagues and family to you. This is extremely valuable, because you're likely to find that client referrals will become one of the building blocks of your service business.

Service can also be interpreted in a whole different way – as service to your community. Providing service to the community can be personally rewarding for both of you. There is always a great sense of satisfaction knowing you are helping others or contributing to the greater good. If through your service business you can also serve your community, you will achieve a different kind of reward beyond profits alone. There is another benefit as well: You'll not only feel good about helping, your service business will become known as a community benefactor, which could repay you in positive publicity, networking with influential members of the community, business referrals and more. Community service is a win for a service business, all the way around.

CHAPTER 7

Managing Growth

G rowth might seem like an obvious goal for any small business. But acquiring too much business and growing too fast may be just as debilitating a problem as starving for business and stagnating.

- Set specific goals for your business and manage the business to those goals.
- Know what you want to achieve in terms of business growth. If growth outpaces capacity, take strategic action to either limit the growth or expand your capacity to support the growth.
- Understand the lifetime value of a client and appreciate the value of loyal clientele. Recognize that renewing and reinvigorating existing business comes at a cost far lower than acquiring new business.
- Don't let little problems escalate into big ones. Keep the emotional burner on simmer and solve problems together.

In the early stages of running a service business, you and your partner are likely to be most concerned about the survival of your business. It is true that a high percentage of small businesses fail in the first several years. Still, we believe that if a service business does the kinds of things we did to acquire clients and keep them happy and engaged, it has an excellent chance of not just surviving but thriving.

Luckily, that's what happened to our business. We officially started accepting clients for our mobile dog grooming business in September 2006. By the end of December 2006, just four months later, we had 34 human clients and Sharon was grooming over 40 dogs. At the end of our first full calendar year, 2007, Bandanas had 80 clients and Sharon was grooming over 100 dogs. Our average monthly income in the first full year of business was double what it was in the first four months. It was exciting to print out monthly reports from our accounting system to see the positive growth.

We never veered from our original marketing strategy. Virtually all of our growth came from very targeted marketing. In fact, most of what we did could be classified as micromarketing. We distributed brochures only in select communities, we had a highly informational website, and we drove the van around. But our biggest success in growing the business came from client referrals.

Despite the wide popularity of social media, we didn't use Facebook, Twitter, or any other form of social media. We didn't advertise and we didn't send out direct mail. We generated sales through referrals, word of mouth, and on the street promotion. Frankly, growing a business this way was a real eye opener to us. With our previous experience running large integrated marketing campaigns for big clients, we never imagined we could rely on such a modest marketing program to grow a business. We were realizing, however, that the best marketing we could possibly have was our reputation for service combined with supportive clients who loved our service.

Now we had another kind of problem, although most business-es would consider it a wonderful problem to have: how to manage the growth of our little service business. In our original business plan, we thought we would run the business in "pre-retirement" mode for five to seven years. We always viewed it as a business we would operate to make a decent profit, but also to provide a life-style that was not as intense as working in a high-powered busi-ness environment. We had had enough of that!

We should point out here that running a small service business could provide a couple with a lot of flexibility. We made a con-scious decision to start a short-term business as a bridge between our busy full-time careers and our later retirement years. We didn't consider ourselves the retirement types. Both of us wanted to be active, stimulated, engaged and involved as we aged. We also wanted maximum flexibility to work when we wanted to work, volunteer, and pursue recreational opportunities. There was an-other practical side to our decision: We knew that, at some point, Sharon would simply get physically tired of grooming. As a result, we had always planned to operate Bandanas for a set period of time and then exit the business.

Boomer couples might find this idea of an interim business very attractive. You may decide to leave a full-time job in your 50s or 60s (or have that decision made for you) and then find it diffi-cult to get another job. Or perhaps, like us, you will plan well enough so that you are able to leave the traditional workforce sooner than most and have the luxury to determine what you want to do next. The beauty of operating a small service business is that you can start it together, with just the two of you, and min-imize your risk by keeping your costs low. If you pick the right type of business, you could probably even choose to run it on a full-time or part-time basis. Perhaps you start out full-time and wind it down to part-time as you age. If your children or other relatives or friends are interested in the business, maybe you bring them in as you phase out. As we said, there is lots of flexibility.

Younger couples can also find opportunity in starting and running a service business. All you need to do is reverse the above scenario. You could start your business as a part-time operation and see how you both work together and what kind of market there is for your services. You might even be able to do this after hours, while you retain your day job. Then, if things go well, you can decide to make a go of the business full-time.

In our case, we conceived Bandanas as a part-time business with an end date in the not-too-distant future. Sharon loved dog grooming, but she anticipated that grooming dogs by herself, all day every day, would take its physical toll. In our original business plan, we projected income based on Sharon working a maximum of three to four days a week, grooming 3 to 4 dogs each day, for a maximum of 16 dogs or so per week. She wanted to reserve one day for grooming dogs at the shelter on a volunteer basis, and another day for personal time. That way, she could leave the weekends free. As a freelancer, Barry was able to keep his schedule flexible to match up with Sharon's.

With over 100 dogs on the books by the end of the first full year, however, sticking to the original plan was a challenge. While some clients used Bandanas only a few times annually, we found that our best clients, a number of whom had more than one dog, were using Bandanas every six to eight weeks. As a result, Sharon often found herself booked up with grooms all day with very little time in between. She was consistently working as many as four days a week all year round, even though there might have been a week here and there when her schedule was lighter. Prior to the holidays, she would be flat out five days a week, sometimes even adding a sixth day, because most clients wanted their dogs groomed prior to Thanksgiving and Christmas.

By the end of our second full year in business, our average monthly income was 50 percent higher than it was at the end of the first year. We realized that we had reached a point at which Sharon really couldn't take on more business without working a jam-packed five days a week. That was not what she wanted to do.

This is when we began to brainstorm about ways to manage our growth. We thought about a number of different possibilities:

1. We could hire an assistant who would accompany Sharon in the van and assist her with basic tasks, such as bathing, so Sharon could concentrate on haircuts. While an assistant might take some of the physical load off of Sharon, it meant hiring and managing another employee, and in the end, this wouldn't reduce the number of grooming days.

2. We could hire a part-time groomer who would essentially job share with Sharon. This person could potentially work three days per week, while Sharon worked three days per week. This was a distinct possibility, but it would mean adding an employee and transitioning some of our clients to a new groomer, which we felt would not be well received. In addition, we would probably have to add even more clients to fill up six grooming days.

3. We could make a conscious effort to expand by adding another Bandanas grooming van and hire another groomer. We could potentially transition Sharon's less active clients to this groomer and actively seek new business. Barry was intrigued by this strategy. He saw the potential for servicing other parts of Asheville and even Hendersonville, a neighboring town. He had also thought about the possibility of franchising Bandanas. Sharon had mentioned to him

that several clients had asked if Bandanas was part of a franchise because they were so impressed with the way we ran our business. Why not make it a reality, Barry thought? But did he really want the headaches associated with trying to build a franchise at this stage of life? We recognized that even adding and managing a second van and a second groomer would be a challenge!

Actually, we chose none of the above. Each of these strategies might have been viable if we were interested in expanding the business beyond its current capacity. That is a legitimate goal for many service businesses – but it wasn't our goal for Bandanas. What we really wanted was to maintain the current level of business and, in fact, pare it down so that Sharon could continue to serve her clients in a high quality way without being overwhelmed and overworked. In order to continue to operate a business that provided the lifestyle we wanted, we had to *limit* its growth.

This may seem counter-intuitive; after all, everything you hear and read about small business suggests that profitable growth should be the first priority. Yes, that's true if you have a long-term business goal, as we had with Barry's first business. But this was different, because we had a short-term goal: Keep the business flourishing for a period of time that was synchronized with Sharon's desire to work as a groomer for five to seven years at most. What we weren't entirely sure of, though, was her exit strategy. That became an important discussion we continued to have, but with no firm immediate solution.

But we did know we needed to limit the growth of Bandanas so it would not grow out of control. We decided to implement several strategies to do just that.

First, we accepted client attrition, which naturally occurs in any service business. You eventually realize that there is a client life cycle and not every client will stay indefinitely. In the first few years, if we lost a client, we made an active effort to replace the business. Sometimes we had taken on a few clients who probably weren't the best fit, either because they were outside our territory or because the dog was too challenging to groom in a mobile environment. We didn't do that anymore; when a client left, we made no effort to replace the business.

Second, we didn't solicit any new business. In fact, we indicated in our phone message and on our website that we had a "waiting list."

Third, we became extremely selective in taking on new clients. In fact, we turned most business away, referring prospects to other mobile dog groomers. We felt no enmity toward other mobile groomers; in fact, we were happy to keep them busy by referring business we didn't want! If we did take on a new client, the client had to fit a very specific profile. They had to be in a tight geographic area as well as have a small dog that required frequent grooming. At the same time, we raised our base price for new clients.

For the most part, it worked, although not perfectly. Our income had leveled off and was about the same in 2008, 2009, 2010, and 2011, but the number of clients had reached around 90 people and 140 dogs. Thankfully, we didn't notice any appreciable drop in business income during the country's "financial meltdown" years. We were happy with the level of business and the income Bandanas was generating at that point.

A BIG KEY TO SUCCESS: RETAINING THE RIGHT CLIENTS

One important lesson we learned over the years was that the real key to service business success is not just client retention, but retaining the *right* clients. Several of Sharon's clients started with her in September 2006 and were still there six years later. More importantly, they were the *right type* of clients for Bandanas: They were in the right geographic area, they valued and could afford our service, and they had smaller dogs that needed to be frequently groomed.

Fortunately, a good number of clients stayed with us over many years, some from the very beginning. These clients represented our pot of gold: They were really the backbone of Bandanas, and even as the business grew, we never forgot how important they were to us. You may have heard of the 80/20 rule, a common business principle that generally holds true across many types of businesses. It basically means that there is a disproportionate relationship between two key variables. It was true for us: While the percentage wasn't exact, we did find that the majority of revenue came from a small subset of loyal clients who used our service time and again, year after year.

Here's just one example of why these core clients were so important. One client who owned two small dogs became one of our very first clients in September 2006, when we started our business. The client had the dogs groomed regularly from the beginning, just about every four weeks. At times the client alternated between baths and full grooms. In fact, Sharon prepared an annual schedule for this client at the start of each year and the client rarely missed a grooming appointment. We kept the client's credit card on file so we didn't even need to get a check for each groom.

When Sharon first began working with this client, the price to groom each dog averaged $45. Six years later, the price per dog averaged $75. This is what the client spent annually with Bandanas from 2007 through 2012:

2007: $ 1,309
2008: $ 1,654

2009: $ 1,817
2010: $ 1,917
2011: $ 2,110
2012: $ 2,134

You'll notice that the amount of money increased each year. Each year, we knew we could depend on this client's continuing business. If you add up the annual amounts, you'll see that this one client was responsible for almost $11,000 of income in six years of doing business with Bandanas. That amount doesn't include indirect income – prospects the client referred to us who became clients, and there were several. This client was still using Bandanas when we sold the business in 2013.

The client example shown above demonstrates the lifetime value of a client and why it is so essential to retain the right type of client for your business. Once you figure out the right type of client for your business, you can figure out ways to keep that client satisfied and make an investment in that client's happiness. Most of the time, client satisfaction is a strong indicator of customer longevity, so you can be fairly confident that a satisfied client will stick around for a while.

There is another good reason to figure out who the right type of client is for your business: so you can get more of them. Once you have a profile of the right type of client, you can seek clients who have the same or a similar profile. This is another basic tenet of direct marketing: Model future good clients after current good clients.

Not surprisingly, in a mobile business like Bandanas, we found that another client just like the one we were servicing might literally live next door. Even if a satisfied client did not directly refer this person to us, there was a good chance the prospect would see the van, since it would be sitting in her neighbor's driveway for at least one hour. Maybe that person would then ask the Bandanas client about the service or, if not, she would call the phone number or visit the website, both of which prominently appeared on the van. Either way, there was a very good chance this person would be interested in learning about our service, if not using it. In fact, when Sharon was out grooming, she would put a Bandanas brochure in neighbors' paper boxes, or in any paper box in the neighborhood that had a sign for an electric dog fence.

By the way, you'll notice that throughout the book, we have referred to our human clients as "she." There's a good reason for that: Most of Bandanas' human clients were indeed women. When we were researching mobile grooming, we suspected this to be the case, and it turned out to be true. We did have some couples as clients, but even then, the woman was the one who primarily interacted with the groomer. Obviously, Sharon was able to relate very well to a female dog owner, in much the same way that a female hair stylist relates to a female customer. Asheville has a significant homosexual population, but only a few gay couples used our service and they were all women.

Earlier, we discussed the concept of acquiring clients at a loss and renewing their business at a profit. Take another look at the client example we used above. We worked hard to acquire that client in the first year. We gave her an introductory discount and performed an extra service here or there to maintain her loyalty. Once that client started using our service regularly and was satisfied, her value as a client continued to grow and increased over the years. Our cost to "renew" that relationship was minimal; we just had to maintain the quality of our service and make sure we were meeting the client's expectations every time Sharon groomed her dogs. Needless to say, this client and all of our most loyal clients got special treatment and recognition along the way. We knew how valuable they were to our business because they were the right kind of clients and we wanted to retain them.

WORKING TOGETHER TO SOLVE PROBLEMS

Part of managing growth is managing problems. You may recall that we discussed in Chapter 4, "Operations," how we divided up our responsibilities, so we could each manage our own little areas of expertise. This is certainly the right approach, and it helped us tremendously in defining who would do what; still, it is almost inevitable that there will be a gray area now and then. Those are the times when a couple needs to remember that the common goal is running a successful business *together* and not let uncertainty or confusion cause a spat. In fact, a little friction might even be a good thing, as long as it doesn't deteriorate into something personal!

Here's an example of one instance that could have become dicey for us if we had not worked together cooperatively to solve the problem. We mentioned in Chapter 4 that some clients paid us by check and, when the client wasn't home, Sharon would leave an envelope so the check could be mailed to us. Sharon had to tell Barry when this occurred so he could manually track when the check was received. The system worked pretty well until one day, Barry overlooked one of the checks. It had arrived in an envelope that was different from the return envelope Sharon had left with the client. This client paid bills electronically, so the payment envelope came from a bank's central processing system While Barry took the check and deposited it with others, as he always did, he forgot to record that the payment was received since it came in a different envelope.

As a result, Barry reported to Sharon that a check had not been received from this client. Sharon rightly wondered about this, since the client had previously always paid in a timely manner. Nevertheless, she agreed that Barry should contact the client via email, as was our standard practice, to politely ask for the payment.

The client responded, indicating that the payment had been sent. Sharon questioned Barry about it, and Barry became somewhat defensive. When he checked, he couldn't find a record of the payment, but when he reviewed the copies of bank deposit slips for the prior month, he found a check amount that matched up with the payment in question. Barry didn't keep copies of checks, so he couldn't be completely sure this particular payment was the payment in question, but he had to assume it was.

Sharon wasn't happy that we bothered a loyal client because of a mistake we had made. She sent an email apologizing to the client. Barry wasn't happy he made the mistake, and he apologized to Sharon, both for the mistake and for getting a little hot under the collar about it. More importantly, after emotions had settled down, the two of us looked at the process together to see if there was a way to make it more foolproof. We modified the process so that Barry started writing each client's name next to the individual checks listed on a deposit slip. Before he made a bank deposit, he would compare any check deposited under a client's name to the "paid" list to make absolutely certain that every payment was accounted for. That solved the problem, and there was never a screw-up again.

We learned an important lesson here. While it is important to trust each other, it is also important to question each other when something doesn't seem right. That's part of the responsibility of managing a business together. In addition, while making a mistake can be embarrassing and even damaging to one's ego, it is essential not just to admit the mistake but find a way so the mistake doesn't happen again.

This example may not seem very significant, but imagine the implications if the mistake would have been blown out of proportion and the two of us had dug in our heels. This could have led to a heated argument – not an inconceivable scenario for a married couple who works together!

Even though Sharon was perturbed, she kept her cool (as she famously does most every time). Barry reacted defensively at first but swallowed his pride once he realized he was wrong. Then we collaboratively worked out a way to solve the problem.

Notice, by the way, that this problem occurred in an area that was Barry's responsibility (receivables) but it *impacted* one of Sharon's areas of responsibility (client service). This is not an uncommon situation. Even when you carefully define each other's areas of responsibility, a problem that happens in one area can affect another area; in fact, more often than not, it will. The key to a harmonious working relationship is to recognize the inevitability that something like this is bound to happen – and to work out a solution to the problem *together* when it does. Mistakes do happen. You might call this part of the *Let's Make Money, Honey* philosophy. After all, "Money" is in the title, but so is "Honey." At the end of the day, you may be in business together... but you also have to respect each other, love one another, and live together!

Consider This...

Business growth is a two-way street. We managed our growth by limiting it, because growing Bandanas larger would compromise our service and mean we would potentially have to add resources. We had a short-term objective for the life of our business so we chose to cap our growth instead of expand. Your objective may be different. Don't be afraid to make decisions based on how you want to manage the growth of your business.

Gain the knowledge you need to identify the right type of client for your business... and then have the courage to turn away the wrong type of client. The right type of client will be the foundation for a lasting successful business. Once you understand the lifetime value of your own "right" client, you will do everything in your power to keep that client satisfied, gain referrals from that client, and retain that client for as long as you possibly can.

Define individual responsibilities for you and your partner, but recognize that overlaps and gray areas exist. When a problem occurs in one partner's area of responsibility, it is likely to affect an area managed by the other partner. Deal with the problem openly and honestly, even if it means having to say, "I made a mistake." Don't allow a little problem to escalate and keep emotions under check. Work together on a solution and move forward as advocates, not adversaries. A little mutual understanding can go a long way. It isn't just about money... it's also about the honey.

CHAPTER 8

When It's Time to Exit the Business

W hen you start a service business together, exiting or selling that business may be the furthest thing from your mind. It is a smart idea, however, to plan for the possibility of leaving the business from the very beginning.

- How long do you want to run a business together? What is your exit strategy? Will you dissolve the business or sell it in the future? Discuss these issues sooner rather than later so you can take the time needed to make smart decisions without undue pressure.

- If you think you want to sell your business, plan for the sale well in advance. Think about how you would transition the business to a new owner. Since client relationships are so important to a service business, spend a lot of time considering how to reassure and retain your clients when the business is sold.

- You never know when a potential buyer for your business may surface. Get an objective valuation of your business. Use a consultant to make discreet inquiries and keep an

eye out for hidden opportunities that may present themselves to you.

- Finding the "right" buyer for your business is just as important as working with the "right" client. The right buyer
respects the business you have built, recognizes the value
of your client base, and welcomes your involvement in a
transition.

While our strategy to limit growth accomplished our objective
of maintaining a stable part-time business, it also had a downside:
Restricting growth meant that we didn't know the real potential of
the business. We always viewed Bandanas as a part-time business
with a lifespan of five to seven years. Yet the fact was, if we limited growth instead of ramping up, we could be creating a less attractive entity if we decided to sell the business. We weren't sure
how we would deal with this dilemma.

In the fall of 2010, we were trying to keep the business at a level Sharon could control. Even so, we were starting to ask ourselves
how much longer Sharon would be able to continue the demanding physical work. She was already experiencing occasional symp-
toms, including sore legs, hands, and back – common complaints
of groomers who have spent more than a decade in the business.
As we mentioned earlier, the holiday season was the busiest time
for Bandanas, and Sharon was beginning to dread the pre-
Christmas schedule that loomed in front of her.

We talked about what we might do to "ease the pain," so to
speak. We both viewed Bandanas as "our baby," a successful business we created together, but we knew it was time to seriously discuss an exit strategy. Sharon was very pragmatic about it – she had
an unwavering loyalty toward her clients and wanted to develop
an approach that would not leave them in the lurch. She felt that

her departure was still a few years away, but she would feel better about it if she set some kind of personal deadline and had an end game in mind.

Before we got too far along, however, we thought it would be prudent to have a conversation with our financial advisor, who was aware of the goal we had set to operate Bandanas for five to seven years. While we didn't have to depend on the income Bandanas generated, it sure was nice to have that revenue to help offset our annual expenses.

We wanted to do a reality check on where we stood. In looking at our assets, investments, Barry's income, and the fact that we were both approaching Medicare and Social Security eligibility, our advisor assured us that, even if the Bandanas income stream were to end in a few years, we could continue to maintain our lifestyle. That was comforting to know, because it meant we could make a decision about Bandanas that wouldn't be influenced by a pressing need for income.

We began to formulate some thoughts about possible ways Sharon could "retire" from Bandanas in about two years. These were the options we considered:

1. *Sell the van and close down the business.*

We thought we could either sell the van privately to a groomer who wanted to go into mobile grooming, or sell it back to the company from which it was originally purchased. Either way, we would be selling the only physical asset of the business and simply closing the business down.

Sharon wasn't too keen on this idea, because she felt an obligation to her clients. She felt uncomfortable with the thought of leaving them without a grooming service. Sharon could of course refer her clients to other mobile groomers, but she was very protective. Her clients had come to know and love the service she provided through Bandanas, so this option wouldn't be ideal.

2. *Sell the entire business to a groomer.*

Another possibility was to sell Bandanas to a groomer. The business sale would consist of the van and all grooming equipment, as well as the grooming software system (including Sharon's detailed grooming notes) and, most importantly, our client list. We believed there was a value to our client list that made it a saleable asset; however, we knew there was no guarantee all clients would continue to do business with a new groomer. To ensure a smooth transfer of the business, Sharon would work with the buyer for a period of time. She would train the groomer on the van and the software, introduce him or her to the clients, monitor the first groom, and be available to answer questions. Barry thought it would be good idea to also train the person in the way in which we serviced our clients – although he knew if the groomer didn't have an administrative assistant, the level of service would probably not be the same.

We both liked this option better than the first one, but we realized that a big hurdle would be the ability of a groomer to purchase the business, so we came up with a third option.

3. *Bring a groomer in as a partner with the intention of selling the business.*

Under this scenario, we would try to recruit a groomer who would work in the business with Sharon with the objective of transitioning the clients to the new groomer. Similar to the second option, the new groomer would be trained on the van, our client service, and our systems. The groomer would gradually take over the business and eventually purchase it from us. As part of the agreement, we would help the groomer with the purchase of the business by allowing the individual to pay us over a period of several years to acquire Bandanas. We felt this would make the difference to a groomer who really wanted to own a business but probably couldn't come up with the money all at once to purchase it.

We liked this option the best, but we also saw challenges with it. We had to find the right person, someone who was willing to work with Sharon for a period of time and could connect with our clients in the same way Sharon did. This person also needed to want to purchase and operate a mobile grooming business. If we were to pursue this option, we recognized that we would be taking a financial risk by allowing the individual to pay off the acquisition in installments.

While a big concern was our clients, we also recognized we had to look out for our own interests. If we were to sell the business, we weren't even sure of its real market value.

Then, Barry remembered that he had enlisted the help of an outside business valuation consultant when he was considering the possible sale of his direct marketing agency. Why not do the same thing for Bandanas? We decided to seek out a consultant, someone who had experience working with small businesses and could also do a valuation of Bandanas.

Thankfully, that person was not difficult to find. Since coming to Asheville, Barry had been volunteering for the small business center at a community college as a brand marketing counselor to entrepreneurs. One of the other counselors at the small business center was an independent consultant who advised small business owners on business, accounting and financial matters. He also did business valuations, so he seemed like a perfect match.

We met with the consultant and told him our story. He assessed our business, discussed our options and advised us about some of the things we might want to do to make Bandanas attractive for sale. He also did an objective valuation. We now had a good idea of what Bandanas was really worth.

The consultant recommended something we suspected we had to do: demonstrate the business had the ability to grow over the next few years so that a buyer would see the potential for future earnings. Of course, we had been pursuing a strategy that was just the opposite – limiting our growth and keeping our income flat – but we recognized that his recommendation made sense. Still, we didn't want Sharon to take on more clients and risk early burn out, and we really didn't want to hire help for her, especially if we were contemplating a sale. So instead, we came up with a compromise that could at least potentially grow our income. In 2011, we started to gradually increase our prices.

We had been servicing most of our long-standing clients at a fixed price per groom that changed only slightly over several years. We began to implement small changes that we felt were legitimate, both to help cover increasing costs and to have a positive impact on income. For example, when the price of diesel fuel spiked, we informed clients we were forced to add a fuel surcharge. We began charging a small fee to those customers who paid us via credit cards; the fee was less than what the bank charged us as a merchant, but at least it offset part of the cost to accept credit cards. We also phased out our policy of giving a 10 percent discount for every sixth groom. We found that regular ongoing clients who were satisfied didn't need an additional incentive to continue using our service.

For new clients, we raised our minimum price. Regardless of the type of dog or the time it took to complete a groom, a new client had to pay the minimum price. When a dog was heavily matted or required a special cut, we charged a higher price. We also discontinued the 10 percent introductory discount we had been offering to new clients.

All of these things did make a difference. By the end of 2012, we had more than a 10 percent increase in income over the prior year, yet we had fewer clients than previously – around 80 people and 115 dogs. In essence, we probably weeded out those clients who were not willing to pay a little more for a mobile grooming service.

Our meeting with the business consultant was a catalyst for both of us to start thinking about how we could reach our goal of selling Bandanas. Just as important, we wanted to find a graceful way for Sharon to exit the business. She really had the best interests of her clients at heart, and any plan we considered had to incorporate a way to make the transition from Sharon to a new groomer as smooth as possible. We knew it would take some time to find the right buyer, and then additional time for a transition.

One important aspect of our moving forward with any kind of sale was keeping that information absolutely confidential. We did not want any client or potential client to know that we were contemplating selling Bandanas because of the obvious negative effect it could have on our current business.

As a result, we couldn't exactly reach out in any public way to groomers or other potential buyers. The consultant said he would make some discreet inquiries on our behalf without revealing our identity. He thought he knew of at least one person who might be interested in purchasing the business as an investment while hiring a groomer to run it. In addition, we agreed to place a few anonymous ads to see if we could generate any interest.

Neither the consultant's efforts nor the ads produced any serious prospects for purchasing Bandanas. These activities resulted in a few inquiries about purchasing only the van, but since we were more interested in selling the entire business, we did not pursue them. We had to regroup and consider our next steps.

AN UNEXPECTED BUYER

In early 2012, a potential buyer unexpectedly surfaced. It all started with a casual conversation. But first, a little background about what led to that conversation.

As we mentioned earlier, Sharon had been grooming shelter dogs on a volunteer basis one day a week for Asheville Humane Society. The society operates the Buncombe County Animal Shelter under contract with the county. It also owns and operates an Adoption Center, situated right next door. Animals are processed through the Shelter and then move over to the Adoption Center. Both buildings form an "Animal Care Campus" that represents a unique public/private partnership.

Stray dogs that arrive at the shelter are often in terrible shape; sometimes they're under-nourished, injured, ill, and/or in desperate need of a bath and grooming. That's when Sharon works her magic. Sharon groomed these shelter dogs in the Bandanas van because there was no adequate grooming facility at the shelter. Even though the shelter was close to her geographic business area, she had to drive the van to the shelter, groom the dogs there, and then drive back. Because Sharon donated her services, we had to cover the cost of gas and supplies without client income to offset these expenses. The bigger issue, however, was the fact that the van had to be thoroughly cleaned and disinfected after grooming the shelter dogs.

There was a small room in the shelter that housed a grooming tub, but it had no grooming tools, supplies, or equipment. Sharon thought it would be great if Asheville Humane Society could get the money to outfit the space as a real grooming room so she could start grooming dogs there instead of in the van.

Barry also volunteered for Asheville Humane Society, but in a different capacity. He wrote the volunteer e-newsletter, was a member of the marketing committee, and he informally advised the president on marketing issues. When Sharon discussed the idea of the grooming room with Barry, he thought it made sense, but he assumed the society wouldn't have the money needed to buy the grooming equipment. He proposed that he have a conversation with the president about the possibility of getting a grant, and Sharon agreed.

Barry met with the president, who was receptive to the idea of outfitting the grooming room; in fact, she knew of a local foundation that had helped in the past and might be able to fund the equipment. She was interested, though, in knowing why Sharon thought a grooming room was so important if she was using the Bandanas van to groom shelter dogs. Barry said Sharon really loved grooming shelter dogs, and she wanted to continue to do so when she retired from mobile grooming some day.

The president perked up her ears. "Oh, is Sharon thinking of retiring?" she asked. Barry said Sharon had indeed been thinking about it. The president then asked if Sharon would be selling the business and Barry said that was certainly a possibility. Barry was completely taken aback by the president's next question. "Would Sharon consider selling Bandanas to Asheville Humane Society?" she asked. Barry didn't quite know what to say, but he promised he would ask Sharon about it.

When we discussed the idea, our initial reaction was very positive. Asheville Humane Society was an organization both of us believed in. We had supported it as volunteers and donors since our arrival in Asheville. We adopted dogs from Asheville Humane

Society and fostered animals for them. What could be better than helping the organization in another way – by selling a business we owned that could generate income for the society for years to come?

We knew the president was a visionary. She helped guide the organization through building the new Adoption Center and establishing a new corporate identity. But never in our wildest dreams did we think that Asheville Humane Society might have an interest in acquiring Bandanas. As we later found out, however, the timing was perfect. Asheville Humane Society was ending a multi-year relationship with the national ASPCA, which included financial support. The organization was looking for new ways to generate ongoing revenue that still fit with its mission.

Bandanas was an established local animal-related business that promoted the proper care of dogs. The business also served an upscale clientele, some of whom already supported Asheville Humane Society. Coincidentally, Bandanas had demonstrated its own support of Asheville Humane Society over the years, because Sharon had told her clients that any tips she received would be donated to Asheville Humane Society. Imagine if Bandanas clients learned that *all* of their grooming dollars would be going to help care for and save the lives of the county's neediest animals. It sounded like a win-win to us.

We told the president we were interested in pursuing the idea. Non-disclosure agreements were signed by key staff members of the organization so further discussions could be held in confidence. In another crazy coincidence, the consultant we had used to do the valuation of Bandanas was a member of Asheville Humane Society's board of directors, so he was able to vouch for the business. While the board was generally receptive to the idea, the organization decided to do due diligence by engaging an outside consultant to place a value on the business.

Things proceeded slowly as we provided the outside consultant with information and he conducted his independent analysis. We had several discussions with the president and a few senior staff about how the business transfer would be made if the sale were to occur. We felt strongly that we both should be involved in the transition. We wanted to ensure that Asheville Humane Society would have everything they needed from us to run the business without any interruption of client service. The staff recognized they had no expertise in grooming or operating a mobile dog grooming business, so they were in complete agreement that we should assist them. In fact, they thought it would be a good idea for us to also help recruit and hire a groomer to replace Sharon. Our assistance in marketing would be needed since the organization wanted to quickly grow the business from its part-time status into a full-time operation.

We recognized that our participation during the transition was essential, but we also felt we needed to be compensated for our time. We worked up a detailed proposal for the kind of consulting relationship we might have, which included administrative training and support, van training, and hands-on time from Sharon. A key part of the proposal was the time we anticipated Sharon would spend working directly with a new groomer.

We came up with a "two groom" plan: She would accompany the groomer on two grooming appointments for every client. During the first appointment, Sharon would introduce the new groomer to the client. Then the groomer would watch Sharon groom the dog. Sharon would talk with the new groomer about the dog's personality and the way the client liked the dog to be groomed. During the second appointment, the groomer would groom the dog while Sharon observed. We felt that the new groomer would appreciate this approach and it would allow enough time for clients to get accustomed to the transition.

As we discussed the components of the proposal, it became clear that we would need to remain involved in the transition for quite some time to cycle through every client twice. Some clients used Bandanas every six to eight weeks, while others got their dogs groomed only a few times each year. We also anticipated that there would be very heavy involvement in the transition on the administrative side for the first several months, but this would taper off later. We thought the best way to proceed was with a one year consulting agreement that would cover the time both of us would have to spend supporting the business and ensuring a smooth transition. Asheville Humane Society accepted the proposal and a consulting contract became part of the final sale.

We developed a detailed time line for the transition, but we didn't anticipate how long it would take to reach a final agreement on the terms of sale. Asheville Humane Society asked a former board member with experience in acquisitions to work with the organization's attorney to finalize the sale with us. We had to work around everyone's schedule, which included a September vacation the two of us had planned and couldn't change.

We had some issues with the first proposal presented to us. We felt the price the organization was offering for the business was somewhat low. In addition, we weren't comfortable with the proposed payout schedule. We made a counter proposal, which had to be reviewed by the board, and then the board came back with a revised proposal. This negotiation took months of time.

Finally, we arrived at terms that were agreeable to all parties. The purchase price was split into two parts, a sum payable upon execution of the purchase, and a payout that would occur upon completion of the organization's fiscal year. The amount of that payout would be determined based on Bandanas reaching certain income levels for the year. We felt this was a reasonable incentive for us, since we were also being paid to consult with Asheville Humane Society for a year and ramp up to a solidly successful full-time business. Our involvement would have a direct influence on the first year of income. The agreement was signed in November 2012, and the sale was executed in January 2013.

THE TRANSITION

The most crucial aspect of the transition was finding the right groomer. Asheville Humane Society wanted to hire the person as an employee but could not afford to pay a base salary that we felt would be adequate for an experienced groomer. We did feel that most groomers would find the society's benefits attractive, but we recommended adding an incentive plan. We suggested that the organization pay an additional amount of money each quarter if the groomer exceeded a target income for the quarter. This meant the organization would only be exceeding the base salary if more money was coming in than anticipated, so there was little risk associated with the incentive. The idea was approved.

Asheville Humane Society advertised the position and we received resumes from groomers who definitely had potential. The best fit for the position, however, was a groomer already familiar to one of the staff who used this groomer to groom his dogs. In fact, the position would report to this staff member! A Certified Master Groomer with twenty years of experience, this groomer was working in a retail environment. Even better, she had previously operated her own mobile dog grooming business. She left mobile grooming primarily because of the headaches of running a business.

When she learned about the position, she liked the fact that Asheville Humane Society would handle the business details and be responsible for servicing the van. She was also receptive to the idea of incentive compensation. She got the job. An unanticipated bonus was the fact that she brought most of her own clients into the business. As a result, Bandanas could more quickly be transformed from a part-time into a full-time business without the need to acquire many new clients.

In November, right after we signed our agreement with Asheville Humane Society, Sharon sent an email to all Bandanas clients informing them of her decision to retire. She indicated she was selling the business to Asheville Humane Society and would remain actively involved in the transition. When the new groomer was hired, Sharon sent another email, along with a letter by mail, introducing clients to the groomer and explaining that she would be accompanying the groomer on the first several appointments.

Behind the scenes, Barry was helping with the administrative transition. He began to train one of the organization's administrative support people on the grooming software system. He continued to check the Bandanas phone line, which remained the same, and monitor incoming emails until these functions could also be gradually transitioned.

Our objective was to keep the business operating without skipping a beat. We wanted clients to get the same level of service to which they had become accustomed. Sharon's client visits with the new groomer went extremely well. After the first few rounds, two things became clear: Clients were overwhelmingly positive about Sharon's replacement, and the new groomer was a great fit in terms of her experience and personality.

Bandanas was on its way to producing income for its new owner. When Asheville Humane Society's fiscal year ended, the income from Bandanas exceeded the highest goal set by the organization's board of directors, so we received the maximum payout. We were right: the sale to Asheville Humane Society really was a win-win.

Obviously, not every exit plan works out this well. When you start a service business, exiting it may be the furthest thing from your mind. Our advice, however, is to think about it up front. By consciously acknowledging that you both plan to exit the business at some point, you may subconsciously be thinking about opportunities that may present themselves when you least expect it. In our case, our involvement with Asheville Humane Society turned out to be an unanticipated path to selling our business. This is an excellent example showing how being active in community can pay off in new and different ways.

Think about exiting your business long before you actually do it. That way, you can work out a plan to help reach that goal. Be expansive in your thinking when it comes to potential buyers. If you care about your clients (and of course, you should), be sure to structure your exit so that you are actively involved in the transition. This will be easier on your clients and the new owner of the business, and it will allow you to leave the business without the common feeling of guilt about deserting your clients.

Consider This...

Deciding to exit or sell a business that you built with your life partner is an emotional ordeal. After all, the business is "your baby." Still, when you start a service business, you need to plan for the inevitability that someday, you are likely to exit the business by turning it over to a family member or friend or selling it to someone else.

Ideally, you will be in a position to "keep it in the family" or sell your business rather than dissolve it, because you will have built its value over time. A wise potential buyer recognizes that a service business tends to be very dependent on the owners' relationship with clients. As a result, it is common for owners to consult with the buyer for a period of time after the business is sold.

In our case, we were not just selling a business, we were selling the relationships Sharon had with her clients. That's why it was so important to find a buyer who welcomed our active participation in transitioning the business. We even participated in hiring the right person to take over Sharon's position. We planned the transition down to the smallest detail. We wanted to make sure that the new owner would be fully equipped to operate the business at the same level of service we provided to our clients for many years. Keeping disruptions and changes to a minimum when a service business transfers from one owner to another will greatly reduce client defections.

When you sell your business, you will probably be just as concerned as we were about protecting the clients you acquired. You feel an obligation to them because of the years of service you provided. While you can't guarantee that a new owner will do things exactly the way you did, you can help by providing access to all of your systems, training new personnel, and conveying everything you know about how you serviced your clients. This will go a long way to smoothing the transition.

We were fortunate that an organization we deeply cared about wanted to buy our business. Sharing a common goal with this organization made us feel very good about selling the business to them. This doesn't always happen in a business sale. When you sell, you should make every effort to sell to the "right" buyer – someone who respects and understands the business you built as a couple, and someone who shares the value you place on your client relationships. In fact, knowing in your heart that the buyer is right for your business may well be even more important than the final sale price.

CHAPTER 9

Can We *Really* Work Together?

I n his 1980 novel, *Lonely on the Mountain*, Louis L'Amour wrote:

> "There will come a time when you believe everything is finished. That will be the beginning."

This wise observation seems like an appropriate way to finish our story and begin yours.

You've accompanied us on a journey we hope you have found interesting if not enlightening. You read about what led to our desire to start a service business as a couple, how we conceived of the idea, how we worked together to make the business a success, and how we eventually sold it. Along the way, we hope you recognized the unique aspects of running a service business, as well as what it takes for a couple to run a business together.

So now, before you embark on your own journey together, take time to do a little serious soul searching. We know, we know, you are anxious to get started, but take it from a couple that has lived through it: Think long and hard before you start a business together. It may surprise you to hear us make such a statement, given the fact we chose that path ourselves. (We wish we had a book like this one to help pave the way.) While we're enthusiastically positive about the conceptual idea of doing what we did, the truth is running a business together simply isn't right for every couple.

We strongly believe that it takes a special breed to be life partners and business partners. Let's review some of the things that made it easier for the two of us to start and run a business together:

1. We knew each other as business colleagues before we fell in love and became a couple. We already had learned about each other's working style and how we would interact in a business setting prior to starting a business together.

2. We started out in business in a kind of client-agency relationship. We had to work together and depended on one another to create marketing materials for the benefit of the company that employed both of us. Later, we further tested our ability to work together when Sharon joined Barry's business. We had to collaborate on new business proposals, work under tight deadlines in a pressure-filled environment, and deal with the "boss' wife" syndrome. These conditions honed our ability to support each other and helped us set limits around each other's responsibilities.

3. Barry had started a successful service business of his own before we started a business together. Using his own money, he grew it from a one-person operation into a multi-million dollar business with more than fifty employees. Doing so was rife with challenges. He already had the battle scars associated with starting and running a service business – so he knew what some of the pitfalls were before we even started a business together.

4. Barry's business was built around his talent and skills, and Sharon supported him by working in his business. When we started Bandanas Mobile Grooming, we realized it would be built around Sharon's talent and skills. This meant Barry had to be able to play a supporting role – not necessarily an easy thing for someone who had run his own business for twenty years. In both Barry's business and Sharon's business, we put egos aside and worked toward a common goal, adapting to roles that were for the greater good of each business.

5. Our personalities and work styles meshed beautifully. We had complementary skills and respected what each of us could contribute to a business. Where Barry could be hot and would often depend on gut feel, Sharon was cool, methodical and pragmatic. Where Barry liked to conceptualize creative ideas and be visionary in this thinking, Sharon focused on details and what needed to be done in the moment. Still, as a couple, we could both kick around ideas and work through details together. We knew how each other would think and could complete each other's sentences. This compatibility as a couple contributed to our compatibility as business partners.

6. We were both marketing professionals. As a result we had a keen understanding of how to build a brand from the ground up and use the right kind of marketing strategies and tactics to build a business. We were trained in the tenets of direct marketing, so we knew it was essential to acquire and retain customers, and we understood the value of building lasting client relationships.

7. Our values and core principles were the same. We both had a high sense of ethics, a dedication to client service, and a desire to give back and serve our community.

8. We had a common interest in animal rescue and volunteered for the same animal welfare organization. We had a love of animals – a shared passion that became central to the business we ran together.

To a certain extent, the compatibilities and commonalities described above might be some of the same things that lead a couple to become interested in each other and form a romantic relationship. Yet some of the things we mentioned are clearly more relevant to forming a successful business relationship.

The combination of the two – the romantic relationship and the business relationship – (the honey and the money) can be at the heart and soul of a partnership that produces sparks in both a good way and a bad way. Here are the two sides of the coin as expressed by professors at the Wharton School of the University of Pennsylvania. The first quote is from Stewart Friedman, practice professor of management, and the second quote is from Laura Huang, professor of management:

> "The trust you have in [your spouse as a co-manager] is greater than you are likely to have with any other business partner in your life. ...It can be exciting to share the joys of accomplishment together. And as a business professional, you're apt to learn more and faster, and to see different perspectives, because you're able to be so vulnerable with each other. ...The big issue has to do with boundaries – how consciously and deliberately the couple manages those, and how mindful they are at tending to the different roles they're in."[4]

> "We assume that [husband and wife-run companies] are a wonderful thing because there are a number of high-profile couples who are still around to talk about their businesses and their marriages and how they make it work. But in general, it may not be a good idea to go into business with your spouse. ...[Couples] haven't necessarily talked about what happens when they need to make changes to the business model, or what the right exit strategy is. They make an assumption because they think they already know and understand the

other person, and they assume they already know his or her perspective. These issues end p destroying many startups, regardless of whether the business partners are married." [5]

Notice that Professor Friedman speaks of the importance of "boundaries," and Professor Huang mentions making "assumptions."

These are two of the areas we found to be most challenging in running a business together.

Boundaries

It might be a good idea to re-read Chapter 4 (Operations) and review how we delineated our responsibilities. We tried to be as specific and detailed as possible in divvying up who did what, basing the decision on who was best suited to which area and tasks. We agreed early on that each of us would have responsibility for certain areas, but part of our mutual responsibility was keeping the other person informed about our respective areas. You could think of this as two managers in a larger business whose departments are interdependent in the way they operate. They are managed separately and independently, yet each manager depends on the other for information to function effectively.

It may seem mundane, but you and your partner should sit down and put on paper every single function of your business and assign one of your names to each. Both of you should keep copies of the list so there is never a misunderstanding. It is also important to determine which decisions can be made individually and which should be made together. For example, any decision about financing your business should be a joint decision; which bills to pay when, however, probably doesn't require dual decision-making.

Another area where boundaries come into play is personal versus business time. Being in business together often makes it difficult to separate your business lives from your personal lives. It is a real comfort to know that you can talk about business matters with your partner after business hours, but that can cut both ways. Take our advice: Hard though it is, try to turn the business switch off when you leave the office for the day (especially if the office is your home). You both need some breathing room away from the business – time for yourselves to talk about other things, to spend time together having fun, and to re-connect with your children, pets, family and friends.

Assumptions

How easy it is to think you know how your partner would answer a question, act in a situation, or respond to a crisis. After all, you know each other so well... right?

Keep in mind, however, that while you may feel you and your partner are always on the same page, it is different in business. If you make an assumption that your partner would handle things the way you would, or would feel the way you do, you are asking for trouble. "I just assumed you..." is the start of a sentence that might have never-ending implications and lead both of you down a very rocky path. False assumptions in business have the real potential to spill over into nasty arguments that could get out of control, damage your personal relationship, and maybe even undermine the business.

The best way to avoid this is to discuss both the little things and the big things as a couple, all the time. Be completely transparent in the way you handle business details and decisions. Ask questions and really listen to what your partner has to say. You know his or her verbal and non-verbal signals well, so read and interpret them, probe when necessary, and make sure you both fully understand each other's position before you walk away from a conversation. The best advice we can give you? Assume nothing.

IS IT RISKY TO BE IN BUSINESS TOGETHER?

There is no doubt about it: There are risks involved for a couple who is in business together. For one thing, personal compatibility doesn't always translate into business compatibility. It often requires being flexible about your relationship, and perhaps even changing the notion of who calls the shots. "Theoretically, you're in a marriage of equals," writes Meg Cadoux Hirshberg, author of the book, *For Better or For Work: A Survival Guide for Entrepreneurs and Their Families.* "But in the workplace, generally one person is in charge. Even if you don't report to your spouse, you are still under them. This lopsided relationship can cause tension." [6]

In our case, Barry had to come to terms with the fact that Bandanas was Sharon's business. Even though he played a role in helping the business succeed via branding, marketing, and administrative support, his role had to be secondary. He accepted that role because it made sense to do so in the context of the business and he knew he could make a contribution that was meaningful without being the boss. Sharon and Barry still made all major decisions together. If Bandanas were a larger organization, one might view Sharon as the head of the company (CEO) and Barry as the operational lead (COO). The CEO and COO in a large company can't function without collaboration, cooperation, and camaraderie. It's the same with couples who are business partners.

In a real sense, couples who go into business together take a double risk when it comes to their livelihoods. "Generally speaking, if one person in a marriage is in the startup phase of a business, the couple relies on the other spouse's income, health insurance and job security to fall back on," says Jeff Reid, director of entrepreneurial studies, McDonough School of Business at Georgetown University. "But if the business is failing and both spouses are 'all in,' it creates an interesting dynamic. When the business isn't doing well, there is tremendous stress on the marriage." [7] Plus, you can't necessarily look outside your own circle of family and friends for financial relief. Reid adds that it is not uncommon for angel investors and venture capitalists to "have a hard rule to never invest in a husband and wife team."

If your business expands and you need to bring on more staff, hiring employees may be problematic. Horror stories abound regarding working for businesses co-owned by life partners, so some job seekers might steer clear of your business. Employees don't want to get caught in the crossfire if there is a battle between the principals; they often think such battles can get a lot uglier than in a traditional business where the two owners are not also living together.

While the impact of working together on the couple's home life may be obvious, this is another type of risk, and a very personal one. It can take a toll that, for some, is too high a price to pay. The relationship has to have a solid foundation to withstand the pressures of co-owning a business. Wharton School professor of management Nancy Rothbard says, "People who do this successfully as couples tend to have a very strong base and marriage to begin with. ... Even though they are spending all their time together, they are both really interested in what is going on with the business. It makes for an incredibly strong marriage. And it can also make for an incredibly strong family." [8]

So after reading this far... do you still have a burning desire in your gut to work together – or is that feeling more like a large dose of indigestion? Seriously, despite all the warnings, we knew we could do it. We had the basis for a solid partnership so we took the plunge. We proceeded with a lot of self-confidence in our ability to make it work. If you believe you can make it work, then we encourage you to go for it.

To help you minimize your risks, we have created three tools:

1. *Business Compatibility Assessment*

The Business Compatibility Assessment is designed to help you do a reality check on your compatibility as business partners. You'll respond to statements individually and then compare your responses to each other to help determine if you have compatible personalities and work styles.

2. *Skills Inventory Checklist*

The Skills Inventory Checklist is a checklist you complete together to assess what specific skills you both bring to the business. If important skills are lacking between the two of you, you should plan to contract outside sources with expertise in those skill areas.

3. *Service Business Startup Checklist*

The Service Business Startup Checklist is a basic checklist of the first steps you need to take when you start a service business.

Business Compatibility Assessment

Instructions: Each partner should take this assessment separately. No cheating: Go into different rooms to complete the assignment! Assign a value of 1 to 5 for each of the statements as follows: 1=Strongly Agree, 2=Agree, 3=Neutral, 4=Disagree, 5=Strongly Disagree. Circle the number that best represents your response to each statement.

1. I consider every aspect of a situation before I make a decision.	1	2	3	4	5
2. I make a decision quickly even if I don't have all the facts.	1	2	3	4	5
3. I usually won't make a decision without consulting others.	1	2	3	4	5
4. I prefer making a decision alone.	1	2	3	4	5
5. I'm happy to let someone else take charge.	1	2	3	4	5
6. I like to take charge and be in control.	1	2	3	4	5
7. I don't like to make waves, so sometimes I may not say what I really believe.	1	2	3	4	5
8. I'm not afraid to speak my mind, even if what I say might not be popular.	1	2	3	4	5
9. Even if I have an opinion, I can be persuaded by others to think differently.	1	2	3	4	5
10. I stick to my opinion no	1	2	3	4	5

matter what others may think.					
11. I need structure and routine when I work and would rather follow a detailed plan.	1	2	3	4	5
12. I can figure out how to do something even if there are no instructions.	1	2	3	4	5
13. I don't like to feel pressured when I'm working.	1	2	3	4	5
14. I work well under pressure when I'm working.	1	2	3	4	5
15. The busier I get, the more tense I become.	1	2	3	4	5
16. Having lots of things to accomplish doesn't make me nervous.	1	2	3	4	5
17. I prefer to work with others as part of a team.	1	2	3	4	5
18. I'm perfectly comfortable working by myself.	1	2	3	4	5
19. I am more comfortable executing someone else's ideas.	1	2	3	4	5
20. I consider myself to be a conceptual thinker.	1	2	3	4	5
21. I like to work with facts and statistics.	1	2	3	4	5
22. I am more comfortable with feelings and instinct than with analyzing data.	1	2	3	4	5
23. I consider myself a "go with the flow" type of person.	1	2	3	4	5

24. I consider myself a "get up and go" type of person.	1	2	3	4	5
25. I can be accommodating of others and I can easily compromise.	1	2	3	4	5
26. I like others to see things my way.	1	2	3	4	5
27. I generally trust people and believe they are honest and sincere.	1	2	3	4	5
28. I can be skeptical of other people's motives.	1	2	3	4	5
29. I know my partner may see things differently from me and that's okay.	1	2	3	4	5
30. I assume my partner will see things the way I do.	1	2	3	4	5

Analysis: The above statements were made up of pairs. The odd-numbered statements represent a personality type of someone who generally is a more methodical, pragmatic, detail oriented, conservative, trusting team player who might like a less intense work environment. We'll call this type "Cool." The even-numbered statements represent a personality type of someone who generally is a more instinctive, conceptual, aggressive, independent person who thrives on pressure. We'll call this type "Hot." Most people have qualities of both Cool and Hot personalities. Neither Cool nor Hot is good nor bad, just different.

When evaluating your answers to these statements, the more you strongly agree with odd-numbered statements, the more likely you are to lean toward Cool. The more you strongly agree with even-numbered statements, the more likely you are to lean toward Hot.

Compare your answers to your partner's answers and see whether you or your partner lean more toward Cool or Hot. If one of you is predominantly Cool and one is predominantly Hot, you are likely to have good business compatibility. If you are both Cool, you can probably work well together but you may have to figure out ways to motivate one another. If you are both Hot, you may have to be prepared for some amount of sizzling conflict, and you may both have to leave your comfort zone when it is necessary to compromise.

Skills Inventory Checklist

Instructions: Complete this checklist together. One of you should respond as "Partner 1" and the other as "Partner 2." Each of you should review the list and put a check mark next to the skills you have. Define "skill" to mean something in which you are accomplished or proficient. If neither you nor your partner has a particular skill, think about the importance of that skill to your business. If you consider it very important, you should either learn it as best you can, or seek and contract an outside source with expertise in that skill.

SKILL	PARTNER 1	PARTNER 2
Starting a business		
Managing a business		
Writing a business plan		
Conceptualizing ideas, products or services		
Personnel management		
Work-flow management		
Accounting and financial management		
Budgeting		
Business negotiating and contracts		
Advertising		

Marketing/marketing research		
Sales		
Customer/client service		
Data analysis		
Research		
Business writing		
Creating/making presentations		
Internet/web/social media		
Use additional spaces below to list other skills you may have or need in your business		

Service Business Startup Checklist

Instructions: Use this as a checklist of items that need to be completed in order to start your service business. Check the item when it is completed. Be sure to research requirements for starting a business in your own town, city, and state since local requirements may vary.

ITEM	√
Create a business name and check name availability with state and federal trademark offices; trademark if it is a unique business asset	
Check web domain availability; register name through an authorized web domain registry service	
Determine a business structure (partnership, corporation, LLC) and file required state forms* (Consult attorney/accountant as needed)	
File your name with local/state governments and apply for any permits that may be required	
Apply for a federal EIN (Employee Identification Number) – check IRS to determine requirements	
File with state department of revenue if payment of sales tax is required in your state	
Write a business plan, including income projections and startup capital required	
Secure startup capital (self-funded or outside sources)	
Determine business location; procure equipment, software, and services needed, including phone number and email address	
Create brand identity and materials: logo, stationery, website, etc.	

* If you hire employees or contract workers, you may be required to file other federal and state forms as well.

Consider This…

At the risk of sounding like marriage counselors, we can tell you that a strong relationship built on mutual trust is the foundation for a successful marriage as well as a successful business partnership. If you decide to start and run a business together as a couple, trusting each other will pervade every aspect of the operation: the idea you conceive, the business plan you write, the capital you raise, the marketing you execute, the clients you acquire, the business you operate, and the service you provide.

In addition to trust, you'll come to learn that you must interact with your partner in a different way. Caring for and loving each other doesn't automatically translate into business compatibility. In fact, having a personal relationship can sometimes cloud your business judgment. You will have to maintain a certain distance as business partners and learn how to make objective decisions together without emotional entanglements. You will have to become accustomed to each other's work styles, which may be very different. You will have to be honest and open about what you don't know and learn how to complement each other's skills. You'll need to learn how to pass the power ball back and forth without one of you being in control all the time. One partner's strengths should make up for the other partner's weaknesses.

The Business Compatibility Assessment and Skills Inventory Checklist are designed to help you understand and appreciate your own and your partner's unique personalities and work styles, as well as the skills each of you brings to your business.

Use these tools to help you know yourselves better and improve your chances for business success.

Lessons Learned

Writing *Let's Make Money, Honey* was really a gift for us. It gave us the opportunity to relive the joy and excitement of starting our service business. It also made us think about the lessons we learned individually and as a couple. While there are many positives about running a business together, most of all it is one heck of a joint learning experience!

So in this final chapter, we leave you with some of the most important lessons we learned in the hope that they offer some guidance and help make your business journey as fulfilling as ours.

Lesson 1: Share a Passion

We were very fortunate in that we shared a passion for animals. We had both owned dogs growing up, and we continued to own dogs throughout our married life. Sharon's love for dogs led to her change her career and become a professional groomer; Barry's love for dogs led him to become a volunteer for a humane society and also start a local dog blog. Our shared passion was the basis for the service business we started. The common bond we shared made it that much easier to work together.

We also shared a passion for running a high quality business centered around excellent service, regardless of the specific service we provided. We had been steeped in the principles of direct marketing, a discipline whose singular focus was the customer, and we had first-hand knowledge of what it meant to provide superior client service through our experience in the direct marketing agency business. Putting the customer first and offering outstanding client service became core principles of the business we started.

We liked the idea of helping people by offering them a service they valued. We liked to make clients feel special. And we liked being able to translate that into a business that could be successful and profitable.

Sharing a passion with your partner will go a long way to increasing your chances of business success. But keep this in mind: Just because you have a shared passion, it doesn't necessarily mean you have a viable business idea. That passion must be applied to a **service that people want**. Identifying a suitable audience that wants to use your service is crucial. That's why it is essential to develop a business plan before you launch a business. Yes, passion is important – but lots of people who are passionate about something might never be in the position to turn their passion into a sustainable business.

Lesson 2: Put Your Past to Work for You

Chances are you and your partner worked for other people and organizations, either individually or together, before starting your own business. This is certainly the case if you are starting your business later in life. What lessons did you learn from your past experience? What skills did you hone? What would you have done differently if you had owned the business instead of working for someone else? Take everything you learned from your past work experiences – both the failures and the successes – and bundle it all together. Then put your past to work for you in your new business.

We had the luxury of working together in two business settings before we started working together in our own business. We both worked for the same company and interacted as colleagues. Then, after Barry started his own business, Sharon joined him as an employee. We not only learned how to work together, we also learned how to maintain a distance between our personal lives and our business lives (not always successfully!). These earlier experiences were invaluable in testing our mettle and proving to ourselves that we had the ability to co-exist in a business setting.

You and your partner may not have directly worked with each other before starting a business together, but that's okay. You probably have a pretty good idea what your partner has experienced in his or her work life. Put that intelligence to good use when you start your own business.

Keep in mind that your past also includes more than just work experience. What have you done outside a traditional job that could be valuable in starting and running a business? Maybe you volunteer in a non-profit organization and you have learned something there that you could apply to running your own business. Maybe you coach kids in a sports team and you could use the leadership skills you acquired. If you participate in sports, your competitive spirit will be helpful. If you have an exercise regime, you are familiar with endurance, another plus. If you participate on volunteer committees, on boards, or in civic activities, the interactions you have in those environments will probably help you in business. Your hobbies might reveal interests and abilities that can be leveraged in your business. The point is, the many facets of your life, both business and personal, should come together on your behalf so you can put all of your talents, skills, and energy into your own business.

Lesson 3: Trust and Support Each Other

Starting and running a service business together will undoubtedly have lots of highs and lows. To manage these ups and downs, you need to keep yourselves grounded. In the greater scheme of things, you want the business you operate as a team to enhance rather than detract from your personal lives. It should fulfill a personal dream both of you have and take your relationship to a new dimension. Sure, running a business will be challenging and at times overwhelming, but it should also be fun and rewarding.

The day-to-day stress and strain of running a business is undeniable. Working together in a high-energy environment sometimes takes it toll on a personal relationship. Disagreements can occur, mistakes can be made. Don't let these flare into serious arguments, personal accusations or attacks. Forgive and forget. Hold each other to a high standard, but recognize that you are both human. Support one another, especially if things don't go the way you planned. At the end of the day, you still have to co-exist peacefully.

One hidden reality of running a business with a loved one often goes unmentioned: Sometimes couples put their personal hats on and carry issues from their home into the business without even realizing it. Here's an example: Suppose you both are in the midst of a fairly serious discussion about your personal finances, particularly your expenses. Perhaps some monthly bills are causing you to be stressed out, or maybe you're in the midst of refinancing a mortgage or talking about buying a new car. Maybe you haven't exactly been seeing eye-to-eye in talking about these things.

Take this piece of advice: It is best to leave these issues where they belong – on the home front. Still, unconsciously, this discussion may rise to the surface during business hours and manifest itself in an unintentional way. If, for example, you are both irritated about the discussion, don't be surprised if you or your partner suddenly reacts to some business decision in an emotional way that seems to come out of left field. What probably happened is that the business decision itself wasn't the real problem, it was the emotion of the underlying personal discussion that reared its ugly head at the wrong time. This is the kind of thing that occurs unintentionally, but the consequences can be significant if both of you dig in and hold your ground. It is probably best to simply ignore it.

There are many such examples of how running a business together will test the strength of your relationship. If that relationship is built on mutual trust, you will know you can put your faith in your partner. After all, if you can't trust your partner, who can you trust? You will find it comforting and reassuring that you and your partner can meet even the toughest business challenge together.

Lesson 4: Stay True to Your Goals

We are both list-makers – we tend to write down the things we have to accomplish, prioritize them, and cross them off as we accomplish them. Part of this somewhat obsessive behavior probably comes from having worked in deadline-oriented businesses for most of our professional lives. List-making was helpful when we started and ran our business, not just for day-to-day tasks, but for goals as well. Writing down our goals together was our way of internalizing them and making sure we could achieve them. Writing them down made them real. This is a common technique you've probably read about in motivational books.

We set goals for lots of things: when we would start the business, how many clients we wanted to acquire, what income we wanted to achieve, and even how many years we wanted to run our business. In each case, we tried to make sure the goals were realistic so we could stay true to them. While it is always good to set an aggressive goal that makes you have to stretch a little, setting an unrealistic goal – one you can't possibly achieve – is counter-productive. You don't want setting goals to become a fruitless and demoralizing exercise.

We learned that there is a fine art to setting realistic goals. You want to push yourselves to reach for the stars, but still keep your feet planted firmly on the ground. It's also a good idea to be as specific as possible in setting a goal. It is much better, for example, to set a specific monetary goal than just say you want to make a profit. It is perfectly okay to have short-term goals and long-term goals, but typically, the short-term goals tend to have tighter parameters and more specificity, while the long-term goals are somewhat less defined.

Whether short-term or long-term, goals still need to be realistic. One way to know if goals are realistic, or at least well defined, is to make them measurable. You should be able to measure the outcome of a goal using objective criteria so you know whether or not you succeeded in accomplishing that goal.

Lesson 5: Know What You Don't Know... and Then Learn What You Don't Know

When you run a business together, you quickly learn there are things you know and things you don't know. In addition, each of you is good at some things but not others.

A truly accomplished expert in a particular field will often tell you he or she still has a lot to learn. Experience has a funny way of teaching you that the more you know, the more you still have to learn.

Learning what you don't know and then figuring out how to make up for that lack of knowledge is actually part of the joy of running a business. In the best possible scenario, you and your partner complement each other perfectly. There is nothing wrong with having a deficiency as long as your partner compensates for it. In our case, we already knew a lot about each other's weaknesses and strengths, but even so, working in a business together brought those strengths and weaknesses into sharper focus.

We quickly realized that there were some things we simply didn't know very well. We had to learn them as part of running our business, even if they were out of our comfort zone. For example, when Barry ran his own firm, he had others managing the financial side of the business, but in our business, he had to do budgets, manage expenses, record income, and forecast sales without the aid of staff. Sharon had worked with grooming equipment before, but she never had to deal with the various systems in a mobile grooming van, or with maintaining the van itself. Now she not only had to learn the ins and outs of all of the equipment, she also had to learn how to troubleshoot when something went wrong.

We made a concerted effort to learn everything we could in our particular areas of responsibility. When we didn't know something, we took pains to learn it as quickly as possible, or find someone else who had the knowledge we needed.

We always maintained a positive attitude toward learning, even if it was frustrating to have to learn on the job. The business doesn't stop even if you don't know how to do something.

But it's really all about attitude. For us, it was always good to learn something new, because it meant we would be that much better at servicing our clients. Learning, after all, is a way of growing that can bring richness to your business and your life. If we learned something new, we were anxious to master it, because we knew that having a new skill would help us run a more efficient business. Having a positive attitude toward learning, and being unafraid to ask questions when you don't know something, is a key to business success. It certainly is a lot more pleasant than being intimidating by not knowing something and suffering the consequences.

Lesson 6: Be Prepared for Something to Go Wrong (Because it Will)... but Don't Panic

Lesson 6 was surely one of the hardest for us to learn. Both of us like to be in control, and we both also have something of a perfectionist streak in us. Feeling competent is important to us. As a result, you can imagine how stressful it was for us when something went wrong.

But we learned, sometimes painfully, that you have to expect something will go wrong once in a while. If you acknowledge this and prepare for it, you will be much better off. In our business, more often than not, that something was related to a van malfunction. While we both received hands-on training from the company that outfitted the van, there is nothing like the real-life terror of having a system fail, right in the middle of grooming a dog. It did happen, although thankfully not very often.

Early on, when there was a van mishap, Sharon would call Barry, who would drop everything and rush to wherever she was to see if he could help her solve the problem. After a few such emergencies, however, Sharon began to learn more about how the grooming systems and the van operated and how to avoid and even anticipate problems. She learned which things she could fix herself, which ones needed Barry's help, and which ones required a quick call to the van company. Over time, we were actually able to fix most minor things ourselves, and it became a real victory for us; in fact, Barry, who is not particularly mechanically inclined, was extremely proud of himself when he successfully swapped out a faulty water pump!

We quickly found out that when things do go wrong, you can't panic. Freaking out really is not productive. You have to maintain your composure, calmly analyze the problem, and do the best you can to solve it – or get help when you can't solve it. Sharon was always honest with clients when she ran into a problem that caused her to reschedule grooms. More often than not, the clients were understanding.

One time, for example, we were hit with several days of extremely cold weather. At night, the temperature went down into the teens, which was highly unusual for our area. Because the van was kept outside at a storage facility, we ran a heater inside the van all night to make sure the water in the lines and the tank wouldn't freeze. Well, one night, the heater didn't do an adequate job, and the next morning, Sharon found that the water lines were frozen. After a frantic call to Barry and then to the van company, we realized it was going to take some time for the problem to be fixed. We had to run heaters for several hours, as well as run a hair dryer directly on the line that had frozen. Obviously, Sharon couldn't complete her grooms that day, so she called those clients with appointments, explained the situation, and said she would call them again to reschedule as soon as we could fix the problem. Not only did the clients understand, but many of them sympathized, since they had neighbors whose pipes had frozen, too.

We just had to work through the problem, not freak out about it, and keep going.

Lesson 7: In a Service Business, It Really is All About Service

We devoted an entire chapter in this book to "service." Honestly, we could have written a whole book about it.

Maybe it's self-evident, but when you are in a service business, your most important product is the service you provide. Regardless of what you actually deliver to the client, the manner in which you provide that service makes all the difference in the world.

We may have operated a very small business, but to us, that business needed to provide a level of service that was no less than that of a world-class service company. In this case, size *doesn't* matter – the quality of the service does. That meant knowing our clients very well, understanding what they (and their dogs) needed from us, and delivering it in a high quality manner, consistently, time after time.

We are students of customer service and admire those companies that use service to set themselves apart from others. Both of us, for instance, are enthusiastic customers of Amazon.com and have been for years. What truly continues to amaze us about Amazon, as marketing professionals, is their ability to provide exceptional personal service to each one of their millions of customers.

Amazon demonstrates its service day in and day by virtually always having the product you want at an attractive price and delivering it when you want it. Amazon's order acknowledgment and fulfillment system keeps you fully informed of exactly when you can expect delivery and of any unanticipated delays. The recommendation engine, pioneered by Amazon, serves up other products you may be interested in based on your purchase. These are all elements of exceptional service that distinguishes Amazon from most other companies.

Some may say Amazon is an online bully that stifles competition, but they have managed to exceed our expectations every time. This, to us, is what customer service is all about: not just meeting customer expectations, but exceeding them.

Even though Amazon is an online behemoth and our business was just a speck in comparison, we looked to Amazon's customer service principles as the model for exceptional customer service. Tiny though we were in comparison to Amazon, our attitude toward service was the same. The service we provided was made up of several components: maintaining a lot of accurate information about our clients that we could put to good use, professionally communicating with clients both prior to and after the service was provided, using high quality grooming products and offering a great service in a high performance van, having an experienced, personable and professional individual who performed the service, and meeting or exceeding each client's expectations.

Even with this attitude, however, we noticed something that occurred after several years in business. Sometimes you can become complacent. Paradoxically, you tend to take for granted your most valued clients – the ones with whom you do business repeatedly. You assume, after a while, that they'll just keeping coming back. That makes it easy to slack off just a little bit. You actually may tire of them, because you provide the same service over and over and again and it can become somewhat boring. A new client, on the other hand is fresh and different, so that client may seem more exciting.

Be wary of this! It is a very dangerous mistake that businesses make. In fact, even large companies are guilty of treating their existing customers with benign neglect while they offer prospects special incentives and handle new customers differently. Think about how that makes you feel as an existing customer!

Most businesses tend to have a relatively small percentage of clients – typically about 20 percent – accounting for the majority of the revenue. It is essential to identify this handful of clients, continue to meet their needs, and keep them satisfied. These core clients deserve special treatment for their loyalty; they are really the backbone of the business. It is their ongoing support and referrals that make all the difference. Never make the mistake of taking them for granted. Without these core clients, there would be no business.

We tried to demonstrate that we cared about our clients in each and every interaction with them – before, during and after each "service call" we made. Sure, not every client is a pleasure to deal with, and some of them can be quite demanding. But we always reminded ourselves that without our clients, we would have no business, so we took pride in serving their needs. That not only made our clients feel good about Bandanas, the company we built ourselves, it made us feel good about owning and operating a business together. We took pride in the little business we built and the service that our clients valued.

In the end, it really is all about service.

Afterword

Our small service business was the third time we had worked together, but it was the first time we owned a business together. We discovered that, for us, nothing could beat co-owning a business. It gave us the ability to build something from the ground up, face the challenges of starting and running a business as partners, and apply all of our previous experience and individual skills to making our very own enterprise successful.

As we look back on the business we started, operated, and eventually sold, we take a great deal of pride in what we accomplished together. While we can't promise every couple that they will get the same kind of satisfaction we did out of running a service business, we strongly encourage couples who believe they can be compatible in business to pursue their dream.

There isn't one right way to go about it, or one right time to do it. Some couples may find it more practical for one to start the business while the other is working elsewhere, joining forces after the business gets off the ground. Others may decide to jump in together from the very start. For some couples, the perfect time to start a business may be before raising a family. Others may want to strike out on their own after being employed by other companies. Losing employment or deciding to leave a job later in life could prompt a couple to start a business. Some might use a partnered business as a fresh opportunity to deepen a relationship by mixing personal and business lives. Or maybe operating a business together represents a joint encore career. If you are both completely committed to the idea, you will know when the time is right to get started.

Whenever you decide to start your service business, it is our hope that *Let's Make Money, Honey* will help you avoid the pitfalls and help guide you to much success.

Resources

A huge number of resources are available to anyone who wants to start a business in the United States. In order to make this section pertinent to the theme of the book, we have selected only current resources we felt are most appropriate for couples interested in starting service businesses. The resources are organized alphabetically by subject area. Internet searches are likely to uncover many more resources. Website addresses are current as of publication. (*http://* has been removed from website addresses.)

Business Plans

Books

Business Plan Kit for Dummies, Steven D. Peterson, Peter E. Jaret, Barbara Findlay Schenck, For Dummies Books, 2013

Business Plans for Dummies, Paul Tiffany, Steven D. Peterson, For Dummies Books, 2011

How to Write Your First Business Plan, Boomy Tokan, CreateSpace, 2012

The Right-Brain Business Plan, Jennifer Lee, New World Library, 2011

Writing Winning Business Plans, Garrett Sutton, RDA Press, 2013

Software

BizPlan Builder

Business Plan Maker

Business Plan Pro

Plan Write for Business

Ultimate Business Planner

Financing and Microlending

Websites

www.angel.co/

www.firstround.com/

www.fundersandfounders.com/

www.sba.gov

www.venturehacks.com/

Microlending Websites

www.crowdcube.com

www.fundable.com

www.indiegogo.com

www.kickstarter.com

www.pubslush.com

www.rockethub.com

www.rockthepost.com

Books

Business Funding Secrets, Boomy Tokan, Amazon Kindle Publishing, 2013

Get Your Business Funded: Creative Methods for Getting the Money You Need, Steven D. Strauss, Wiley, 2011

The SBA Loan Book: The Complete Guide to Getting Financial Help Through the Small Business Administration, Charles H. Green, Adams Media, 2011

General Information for Small Businesses

AARP
AARP specializes in helping individuals 50 years of age or older. This portion of their website is about working after retirement.

www.aarp.org/work/working-after-retirement/

AllBusiness.com
A website with information and news for small businesses.

www.allbusiness.com/

Entrepreneur
This leading publication/website is packed with information about startups, running and growing a business, financing, and more.
www.entrepreneur.com/

Fast Company
A trendy magazine focusing on fast-track companies.
www.fastcompany.com/

Forbes.com
This resource is of particular interest: "100 Best Websites for Entrepreneurs"
www.forbes.com/pictures/ekij45ihjj/100-best-websites-for-entrepreneurs-4/

Home Business Magazine
www.homebusinessmag.com/

Inc.
Another publication/website that serves the needs of small businesses.
www.inc.com/

NFIB My Business
Online publication sponsored by the National Federal of Independent Business.
www.nfib.com/business-resources/mybusiness-magazine/

SBA

The United States Small Business Administration (SBA) is likely to be one of your best resources for all kinds of information.
www.sba.gov

SBCN (North Carolina)

This resource is included as an example of one state's Small Business Center Network. These Small Business Centers are located at the state's community colleges and sometimes include business incubators. Do an Internet search to see if your state has a similar network.
www.ncsbc.net/

SBDC

This is the central website for Small Business Development Centers located around the country that offer free counseling and other services for small business.
www.asbdc-us.org/

SCORE

SCORE has helped millions of small businesses for fifty years with free counseling, mentoring and workshops.
www.score.org

The New York Times: Small Business
www.nytimes.com/pages/business/smallbusiness/index.html

The Wall Street Journal How-to Guide: Small Business
guides.wsj.com/small-business/

Marketing a Small Business

Books

Building a Big Small Business Brand, Dan Antonelli, SignCraft Pub. Co, 2013

Branding 123, Second Edition, Barry Silverstein, 123 eGuides, 2014

Branding Basics for Small Business, 2nd Edition, Maria Ross, NorLights Press, 2014

Brand Sense – Sensory Secrets Behind the Stuff We Buy, Martin Lindstrom, Kogan Page, 2010

Data Driven Marketing: The 15 Metrics Everyone in Marketing Should Know, Mark Jeffery, Wiley, 2010

Duct Tape Marketing, Revised and Updated, John Jantsch, Thomas Nelson Publishers, 2011

Guerilla Marketing (Series of books), Jay Conrad Levinson, various publishers

Small Business Marketing Kit for Dummies, Barbara Findlay, Schenck, For Dummies Books, 2012

The Breakaway Brand, Francis J. Kelly and Barry Silverstein, McGraw-Hill, 2005

Online Course

Big Brand Strategies for Small Brands, an on-demand online course taught by Barry Silverstein (www.bigbrandstrategiesforsmallbrands.com)

Startups

Websites

www.OnStartups.com

www.StartupLawyer.com

www.StartupNation.com

Books

How to Start a Service Business, Meir Liraz, Liraz Publishing, 2013
Limited Liability Companies Small Business Start-Up Kit, Daniel Sitarz, Nova Publishing Company, 2010
School for Startups, Jim Beach, Chris Hanks and David Beasley, McGraw-Hill, 2011
Small Business For Dummies, Eric Tyson and Jim Schell, For Dummies Books, 2011
Start Your Own Business, 5th Edition, The Staff of Entrepreneur, Entrepreneur Press, 2010
The Startup Playbook, David Kidder, Chronicle Books, 2013

Working Together as a Couple

Articles

"From the Altar to IPO: The Highs and Lows of Married Business Partners,"
knowledge.wharton.upenn.edu/article.cfm?articleid=3177

"How These 9 Couples Mixed Business and Pleasure – and Made Startups Worth Millions"
www.policymic.com/articles/82303/how-these-9-couples-mixed-business-and-pleasure-and-made-start-ups-worth-millions

"Launching with a Loved One? Five Lessons from Successful Startup Couples"
www.entrepreneur.com/article/226778#

"Married to My Small Business Partner"
www.washingtonpost.com/business/on-small-business/married-to-my-small-business-partner-stories-and-advice-from-10-entrepreneurial-couples/2013/02/14/bf73820c-7639-11e2-aa12-e6cf1d31106b_story.html

"Married to the Job and Each Other"
online.wsj.com/news/articles/SB10001424052748703959104576082623914872658

"Together at Home and at Work"
www.nytimes.com/2013/11/17/fashion/rules-for-couples-that-work-and-live-together.html?_r=0

Books

Couple CEO: From the Bedroom to the Boardroom and Back, Scott & Heidi Shimberg, Morgan James Publishing, 2015
Couplepreneurs: Prosperity Through Partnership, Jean R. Charles, Wheatmark, 2006

For Better or For Work: A Survival Guide for Entrepreneurs and Their Families, Meg Cadoux Hirshberg, An Inc. Original, 2012

In Business and In Love: How Couples Can Successfully Run a Marriage-Based Business, Aprill and Chuck Jones, Markowski International, 2002

Inspiring Couples: In Business and In Love, Janell and Rob Alex, CreateSpace, 2014

Sleeping with Your Business Partner, Becky L. Stewart-Gross and Michael J. Gross, Capital Books, 2007

Soulmate Proprietors: How to Run a Business with Your Spouse and STAY Married!, Danelle Brown, Queen Bee Consulting, 2010

You & Your Partner, Inc.: Entrepreneurial Couples Succeeding in Business, Life and Love, Volume 1, Miriam Hawley and Jeffrey McIntyre, Enlignment Press, 2012

Notes

1.   Testimony of Dane Stangler, Vice President, Research and Policy, Ewing Marion Kauffman Foundation, before the U.S. Senate Special Committee on Aging & the Senate Committee on Small Business and Entrepreneurship, February 12, 2014

2.   Family Firm Institute, Inc., "Global Data Points," www.ffi.org/?page=globaldatapoints

3.   Sitarz, Daniel, Attorney-at-Law, *Limited Liability Companies Small Business Start-Up Kit*, Nova Publishing Company, 2010. pp. 31-32

4.   "From the Altar to IPO: The Highs and Lows of Married Business Partners," Knowledge@Wharton, January 30, 2013 (knowledge.wharton.upenn.edu/article.cfm?articleid=3177)

5.   Ibid.

6.   Ibid.

7.   Ibid.

8.   Ibid.

Acknowledgments

Many people helped shape us over the years so we would become good life partners and business partners. It begins, of course, with supportive parents, family, and friends. For this specific journey – starting a service business together – we benefitted from the expertise, vision, and experience of numerous business professionals. We owe a debt of gratitude to Sandra Bromfield, Eric Sneider, Julian Friedman, Sandra Bowers, Mike Sowinski, Katherine Shenar, Jim Fulton, Rick Clark, Sam Craig, the Board of Directors of Asheville Humane Society, and the loyal clients of Bandanas Mobile Grooming Salon.

About the Authors

Barry Silverstein and Sharon Wood have worked together in one capacity or another for over three decades. They have also been married to each other for nearly that long. Silverstein and Wood met while working for a direct marketing firm. Later, when Silverstein started his own direct marketing agency, Wood joined him to direct new business development.

After successful careers in marketing and sales, Silverstein and Wood decided to relocate from Massachusetts to Asheville, North Carolina. That's when they started a small service business together. They sold the business six years later. They proved without question that couples can not only successfully work together, they can start and run a business together. They documented their experience in the book, *Let's Make Money, Honey: The Couple's Guide to Starting a Service Business.*

Silverstein and Wood continue to collaborate as volunteers for Asheville Humane Society. Wood is a retired certified dog groomer who now donates her time and expertise grooming shelter dogs to make them more attractive to potential adopters. Silverstein is a freelance writer and brand marketing consultant. Silverstein is the author of six non-fiction books, including *Business-to-Business Internet Marketing* (the first book written on the subject) and *The Breakaway Brand.* He self-publishes eGuides for small businesses, teaches an online course, *Big Brand Strategies for Small Brands,* and is a volunteer brand marketing counselor at a Small Business Center.

The couple resides in the Asheville, North Carolina area.

About GuideWords Publishing

GuideWords Publishing is a small publisher of quality non-fiction books. GuideWords specializes in the intersection of the very small business and senior markets, aiming to offer active and engaged seniors the information they need to succeed in starting and running small businesses and living productive, fulfilling, financially secure lives.

Let's Make Money, Honey: The Couple's Guide to Starting a Service Business is the company's first book. Word of mouth is so important to a book's success today. If you found *Let's Make Money, Honey* to be of value, the publisher would greatly appreciate it if you would recommend it to others. Please consider posting a positive review online at Amazon.com, BN.com, Smashwords.com, or other sites where you may have purchased this book.

Learn more about GuideWords Publishing and follow our blog at:
www.guidewords.pub

You may also be interested in a series of eGuides published by our sister company, 123 eGuides. These authoritative guides are published exclusively in electronic format to provide maximum value at minimum cost – just $2.99 each. 123 eGuides are designed for today's reader who wants information in a quick, convenient, easily readable format. Each 123 eGuide is intended to provide a functional overview rather than a detailed roadmap. Every 123 eGuide always includes additional resources if the reader wants to learn more. Titles include *On Your Own 123, Branding 123, Product Launch 123, Sales Leads 123*, and *B2B Marketing 123*.

Learn more about 123 eGuides and follow our blog at:
www.123eguides.com

Index